The Millionaire Brain

The Millionaire Brain

◆

Real Secrets of Millionaires

Donny Lowy

iUniverse, Inc.
New York Lincoln Shanghai

The Millionaire Brain
Real Secrets of Millionaires

iUniverse, Inc.

For information address:
iUniverse, Inc.
2021 Pine Lake Road, Suite 100
Lincoln, NE 68512
www.iuniverse.com

ISBN: 0-595-30723-X

Printed in the United States of America

Contents

PREFACE

This publication is designed to provide accurate and authoritative information in regard to the subject matter covered. It is sold with the understanding that the author is not engaged in rendering legal, accounting, financial, investment, or other professional service. If legal advice or other expert assistance is required, the services of a competent professional person should be sought. The information in this book is only for educational purposes and should never be used unless one has first personally consulted with a licensed professional. By reading this book you are acknowledging that you will always personally consult with a licensed professional adviser before making any decisions and that you will take sole responsibility for any decisions that you make. You may read this book for entertainment or educational purposes but you should never use the information without the specific instructions of a professional who knows your personal situation.

INTRODUCTION

Much has been written about the benefits of starting a business. Much has also been written about the risks of starting a business. Among the benefits that we can see is that people who have a business have the best chance of becoming self-sufficient, becoming financially independent, and of attaining millionaire status. We also see that the risks of starting a business are that one could lose all of their savings, they could be heavily in debt, and they might have to start from scratch in their career or, if they decide to start another business, they'll have to make up for lost years if they lose their business.

So we see there are many risks and many benefits of starting a business. Some of the benefits of starting and running a business are not concrete benefits and those benefits still hold true even if someone is not successful in their business. One of those benefits is the ability to have control over one's life. It's the ability to decide for one's self what direction a person wants to take in their life, what it is that they want to be involved with, what pursuits interests them, and what they find satisfying in life. By the running of their own business they're able to have a more fulfilling lifestyle regardless of how much they make because they're going to be involved with doing what it is that want.

When you look at the successful millionaires who run their own business, you'll notice that whether their business is making money or its losing money, or whether they're at the beginning stages of their business, whether if they're already at the stages where they're looking to sell their business, they have a very high satisfaction with themselves because they're involved with a pursuit that interests them. They're actualizing their goals, dreams, and aspirations. They're deciding for themselves what it is that interests them the most, what it is that they want to do, and then they go ahead to formulate a plan that will allow them to spend the majority of their time doing what it is that interests them.

You see, most successful millionaires who are in business for themselves don't set out to become millionaires. What they set out to do is to become involved in a pursuit that will allow them to have control over their lifestyles, that will allow them have more time to spend more time with their families, friends, for their associates, and also to have more free time to pursue activities that they enjoy. At the same time they want to become financially independent so that they have more time and to also have the resources to spend that time with their families and friends, and in whatever other ways in which they best utilize their time. Of course they want to become financially successful, which is more of a side benefit that they'd like to be able to enjoy. You see, if someone sets themselves up to become involved in a business only to make money, they'll have a very difficult time.

As we know, when most businesses start, even if they're making money, it could take considerable time to start making a substantial amount of money. It could take a long time until the business attracts enough customers and until the business has enough revenue so that the business owner will have the financial satisfaction he seeks from running that business. Most successful business owners realize that even if they do make money from their business, it will take plenty of time. So they set for themselves other motivational factors that will help them push ahead and persevere while running their business. They are the same people who will end up running successful businesses that will help them attain millionaire status, so you see then, that millionaire status is a result of having the right mindset and having the right attitude while being involved in business.

Now, the benefits are still there. If someone does persevere and is very persistent in their business and has a very set goal that's clearly discernible so that they know exactly what it is that they're out to do, what it is that they need to do in order to accomplish their goal, and their business does make sense. The business is something which can work out, meaning that the business is well-founded on a solid basis, having been researched and having been found to have a real life potential. As a result of all of these factors, the owner of that business will end up running a business that will make money. The owner of the business, over time will have a very good chance of getting closer to having attained that millionaire status and a certain percentage of business owners who are highly motivated are highly successful and not just financially though. Their attitudes, their perseverance, and their persistence have the ability to weather financial turmoil and other ups and downs of the business cycle. They are the ones who will be able to attain millionaire status.

If you want to become a millionaire business owner, which is possible, especially in the United States, we see that we have the highest percentage of millionaire business owners. If you want to join their ranks, then you need to know what it is that those millionaire business owners are doing so that you are able to instill the morals and the values that they have that you are able to replicate their success systems that they use which will enable you to become very close to becoming a successful millionaire business owner.

1

So, what is the secret of millionaire business owners? What is it that enables them to start up a business, become infatuated with the business, truly enjoy and persevere in the business even when they are ups and downs? We know that it's easy to be involved in a business when the business is always making money. It's actually quite easy because there's money coming in, the person enjoys the ability to make money, they see what they could do with their money, and they're continually becoming involved in the business. But what is it that allows some of the same business owners to take their business to the next step even when their business is making money?

See, while many business owners become satisfied with their level of income, millionaire business owners are always plugging ahead with their businesses and are always looking for ways to increase the earning levels of their businesses. Now most people are usually satisfied at a certain level and even if they want to make more money, there is a certain cap to the amount of work that they're willing to put forth compared to the results that their business is producing. For instance, if someone is involved in a business and is looking to have a six-figure income, and that business owner starts making a hundred thousand dollars from his business year after year, that business owner might be willing to work an extra five or six or ten hours a week to increase his income from a hundred thousand dollars to one hundred fifty thousand dollars and that business owner might be willing to give up his or her weekends to make two hundred thousand dollars for the year, but that is usually the amount of sacrifice that a business owner might make to increase that income. We do see though, that millionaire business owners are able to run businesses that deliver results of upwards of a million dollars per year. There are many millionaire business owners whose businesses give them a net five or ten million dollar salary or earnings per year.

We have to understand what it is that pushes those business owners to always aspire to the next level where they can make more money. On the other hand, most businesses do fail. We know that eighty percent of businesses that are started up in any given year will fail within three years. That also includes businesses started by millionaire business owners.

You'll find that millionaire business owners usually don't become extremely successful in their first business venture, but sometimes it takes two or three business ventures before they actually arrive at the level of success they are seeking. Even those business owners who go through two or three business ventures in order to attain the success for which they're looking will have sacrificed sometimes hundreds of thousands of dollars before achieving their goals. They'll sometimes lose their homes, all of their savings, and have to go heavily into debt. You can see though that those millionaire business owners are somehow always able to eventually succeed. They persevere and eventually always meet their goals. If you read the stories of any millionaire business owners, you'll find that they've had many losses, challenges they've faced at the beginning, and that they didn't have any clear financial successes when they first started. On the other hand, you can see that those millionaire business owners, upon beginning to make money and reaching financial success, continued always pushing to the next level.

We need to know the secret of millionaire business owners. What allows them to persevere through hard times and through good times? When I say persevere through good times, I mean that those same business owners are not satisfied with their level of earnings and are always looking to increase them. They're always looking for ways to move on to the next level. What I have seen from speaking to millionaire business owners and other entrepreneurs, I find that they only involve themselves with businesses that they truly enjoy. What ends up happening is that they only become involved in businesses that are a hobby to them. They want their businesses to give them fulfillment. They're not simply looking for businesses that will make them money. They're not simply looking for businesses that can make them money. They're looking to involve themselves with businesses that excite them; ones that make them stay up at night with enthusiasm. They want to be involved with businesses that excite them so that they'll look forward to starting up the business again the next morning.

The difference between most people who have a job and most people who are business owners is that people who have a job are forced to work at their jobs. They need to go to work day after day because they need to have that paycheck to pay the rent, to pay the mortgage, to pay their car payments, to pay for their children's education. Their fear of losing that job is directly related to their fear of having an inability to meet their financial obligations.

On the other hand, most business owners go into business because they want not only to be able to meet their financial obligations, but also because they want to become financially independent and they want to make enough money to be able to afford the extra's in life, such as going on fancy vacations, buying a second home, or having a second or a third car. Millionaire business owners differentiate themselves from other business owners because they're involved in business not just because they want to become financially independent, which of course everyone wants to become at some point. The reason they become involved in the business is because those are businesses that they enjoy. There are specific areas that they find fulfilling in their lives.

I've met millionaire business owners who are involved in the clothing business as well as millionaire business owners who are involved in the animal business. The business owners who become millionaires through doing the same professions for which other people only receive a monthly paycheck. There are millionaire business owners who apply their teaching skills to their businesses and they become involved in businesses in which the complete aim of the business is to teach. There are millionaire business owners who enjoy counseling and the whole purpose of their business is to provide counseling. There are millionaire business owners who enjoy museums, so the whole purpose of their business is to set up museums or to work in the museum field.

You see, what enables a business owner to attain the status of a millionaire business owner is that they truly enjoy and actually like what it is with which they are involved. What happens is that they get so caught up in their businesses that even when their businesses are not making money these people want to continue being involved in their business because they enjoy what it is that they're doing. And, at the same time when their business starts making money, they decide to be involved in the business and to continue pushing the business to the next level because they're deriving personal satisfaction from running their business.

So for example, take someone who runs a restaurant. If they're a regular business owner, they might be satisfied with seeing that their restaurant is delivering a good profit year after year and that profit allows the owner of the business and his/her family to go on nice vacations, to have a second home, to wear the finest clothing, to drive three or four cars, but what will actually motivate the millionaire business owner who owns a restaurant is the fact that he or she enjoys running a restaurant. She enjoys seeing the reactions of her customers when she presents the latest culinary delights that she has introduced into her menu. She loves seeing the reactions of her customers when they see the innovative designs that she implements in her restaurant. She loves seeing their reactions to how she sets up her menus. She loves interacting with her patrons of her restaurants.

You see, a millionaire business owner will become so involved with his/her business that that once they feel that their restaurant has reached its limitations, they'll open up a second or even a third restaurant, only because they relish so much the challenges of starting up and running a restaurant and taking that restaurant to its height.

Let's say for instance that you want to become a millionaire business owner and you're involved in the restaurant business. What will happen is that you will have initially opened up a restaurant because you love the challenge of finding a location to open a restaurant. You love the challenge of introducing new dishes to the local market that you're serving. You love the challenges of filling your restaurant with happy customers who love coming back to your restaurant. But, then there will be a time when your restaurant will be filled night after night. You'll have a lot of work and many commitments, but you'll also have the staff which will be able to support the work that your restaurant requires. At that point, you'll say to yourself, "Look, the start up challenges have been overcome. I already have a restaurant, the challenges of making this restaurant a valuable restaurant have also been overcome because people are coming to the restaurant, they're patronizing the restaurant, and the restaurant has a good clientele. Then the challenge of having this restaurant become an excellent restaurant that's a big money-maker for the owner of the business will have also been overcome because now your restaurant is making an above-average profit year after year.

Now, if you're a millionaire business owner or you want to become a millionaire business owner, you're going to have to be someone who loves the restaurant business. If the restaurant business is something that excites you, you're going to say to yourself, "Now that I've already overcome the challenges that I had to face in order to open up my restaurant, what I miss is not running a restaurant because I am running a restaurant, but what I miss is the challenges of opening up a restaurant, of introducing new dishes to a new local market. What I miss is the ability to have the challenges of attracting new customers to my restaurant.

Now as a millionaire business owner, you'll find yourself wanting to start a second restaurant only because you miss being involved with all of the facets of starting up a restaurant, and of working with that restaurant to continually increase its business until it becomes financially sufficient enough to attain your goal. What you'll see is that what actually drives you is not the financial results of the restaurant, but the actual being involved with a successful restaurant. Once that restaurant attains a level at which there's a ready supply of support staff operating it, then you're going to miss being involved with what it is that's your hobby, which in this case is starting up a restaurant.

Millionaire business owners are always involved with business that they love. What ends up happening is since that they love every facet of their business they want to have the opportunity to constantly be involved with every facet of that business. There are many facets of a business that only occur at the beginning or at the middle stages of running a business. Once your business reaches the stage of the cycle where the business has already passed all of those opportunities for doing those activities, a millionaire business owner will look to start a second or a third business or even open up a second or a third location simply because he or she loves being involved with those activities. They love looking for new customers and clients. They love marketing their businesses. They love figuring out the prices for their businesses. They love finding the best products or services to match up for their clientele.

Once they have done all of the above, they look for new opportunities to repeat what they have done in the past. That person then falls into a cycle, which is a beneficial cycle, where you end up finding new opportunities to make money and new businesses to start, whether they are of the same type of business or businesses in other areas. The business owner who ends up becoming the millionaire business owner who's only primary motivation is the love of being involved in a business, which is the reason why they have started that business.

If you want to become a millionaire business owner, you need to make sure that the business you're considering becoming involved in is something that you truly like, and is something that if it wasn't business, you would consider doing it as a hobby because you do enjoy doing it so much.

2

Millionaire business owners know that in order to become successful in any field, they're going to need to have a very clear grasp on the subject of their field. A millionaire business owner knows that it's not enough to have a general interest in a field, or even to have a general understanding of a field in order to become successful in it. The millionaire business owner know that if he or she wants their business to become an extremely successful business that produces money year after year and is able to attain a very high level of financial success, then that business is going to have to be in an area that the owner of the business can be considered an expert.

A millionaire business owner knows that while expertise is not enough to guarantee success, without expertise, it is going to be extremely hard to attain any measurable level of financial success. A millionaire business owner knows that in order to be able to attain a very high level of financial success, they are going to need to be able to become an expert at what it is that they're doing, even before they become involved in the business, they are going to have to have a certain level of education in that business or in that area they're looking to enter that will set them above their competition and other people in the field.

For instance, a millionaire business owner who's looking to open up a clothing store for children is going to have to have not only a basic understanding of the children's clothing business, but also a perspective from which to enter the children's clothing business…whether it's from a parent's perspective or from the perspective of someone who's involved in the clothing business. They're going to have to have a very clear grasp on the children's clothing business. They're going to need to know what it is that children wear and during what seasons do children wear certain types of clothing. They're going to have to know what parents' preferences are for buying certain types of clothing for their children. They're going to have to understand the market for children's clothing. What type of clothing do parents buy for children in hot climates and what type of clothing do parents buy for children in cold climates. They're going to have to know whether parents are more concerned with the style, with the quality, or with the price of clothing. These are all factors that cannot be left to guesswork. In order for someone to become successful in the children's clothing business and to become a millionaire business owner in the children's clothing business, they're going to have to have a high level of expertise.

Now a millionaire business owner knows that it's not always possible for him or herself to become an expert in the field. So what they do is surround themselves with experts in the field. They make certain to reach out to people who are experts in that field and try to include them in their business, so that they are able to draw from the positive expertise that the individual brings. In this way instead of they themselves having to become an expert in the field, they're able to have a high degree of knowledge and a high degree of success based on the information that can be provided by the expert with whom they are communicating.

At the beginning, when you first start out your business, you might be very hesitant to want to bring someone else into your business. You definitely might not want to have a partner because on one hand, when the business becomes very successful, you're going to want to be the only recipient of the success of your business, especially at the beginning, when it's a small, growing business. On the other hand, it's going to take time until your business can support two people. So if you're starting your business from scratch and your business will be your full-time occupation, you need to make sure that you're not splitting the profits of your business with someone else since you're going to be depending on the financial production of your business.

Given this information, how do you have an expert join your field? You will have an expert with whom you have either a social relationship or an expert who will be able to benefit from other areas besides having to derive financial results directly from your business. For instance, if there is an expert in the children's clothing business and this expert has a clothing wholesale company and you're considering opening a children's retail store, you might want to tell this expert in the field who happens to be a wholesaler that if he is able to spend the time with you, to sit down with you and to fully explain to you what clothing will sell in what market and what type of clothing will sell during different periods of the year, then not only will you divert all your purchases to him, but that you'll make him your exclusive supplier at least at the beginning stages of your business, but you'll also pass on referrals to him from other children's clothing store owners.

Naturally, as you start running your business, you'll come in contact with people who are also involved in the same businesses in which you're involved. If you can pass the names and numbers of those people as referrals to the wholesaler, he'll be very happy in return to take that time out of his busy schedule to advise you and to provide free consultation to help you succeed in your business.

Millionaire business owners know that in order for them to succeed in their business, they're always going to need to have experts advising them on their business. They know that in order to make sure that these experts are committed to helping them become successful in their business; they're going to need to have something that they're going to be able to deliver in return to the expert that is providing them with advice.

Now millionaire business owners know that while you should always have an expert, the best types of businesses to be involved with are business where they themselves are experts in the field. You see, many people don't realize that regardless of their level of education and the areas in which they are knowledgeable, there is always something in which they're an expert. The key is to discovering in what area they're an expert. If they can discover in what area they are an expert, then they can next examine the opportunities to make money in that area.

A millionaire business owner knows that even though he or she might not be an expert in an area that seems financially very lucrative or in which there is money to be made in every area. A millionaire business owner knows that even if he or she is an expert in a very basic area such as stamp collecting, they're aware that there's a tremendous market in stamp collecting. If that person knows everything about stamp collecting, then they can position themselves to buy and sell stamps and to become millionaires through the business of stamp collecting. If the millionaire business owner is an expert in collecting old paintings, then this person could go ahead and find sources to purchase the paintings since they will already know the value of the paintings, they will know which paintings are worthwhile and which paintings are not worthwhile to buy. They will also know which paintings have the highest level of demand in the market and will able to become millionaire business owners in the painting business.

Now, you will need to examine what areas in which you could be considered an expert. Believe me when I tell you that it doesn't matter in what area you're an expert. It could be something as mundane as knowing the best type of pet food to knowing the best type of floor wax needed to clean your floors. It really doesn't matter in what are you're an expert because every area has people who are millionaires making money in that area. Every area has its own millionaire business owners who are making money year after year.

Let's look at the two examples that I gave you. One example was becoming an expert in pet food. You might have become an expert in pet food inadvertently because for years you have had to go to the supermarket and decide for your animals which are the best pet foods for giving your animal energy and keeping your animal healthy. After developing a strategy and an ability to find the best pet food, you could take that ability and those strategies that you've learned and use them in the business marketplace. A millionaire business owner would go ahead and set up a store selling pet food to pet owners that wanted a high level of quality and wanted pet food which clearly met the needs of their pets. A millionaire business owner would position himself or herself to make sure that they could supply the type of pet food and the type of expertise and information that would encourage pet owners to come to his or her store to purchase their goods. You can see that there are actually million dollar chains, multi-million dollar chains operating in this country on a national basis and there are even international pet food chains of which the sole purpose is to sell pet food and pet supplies to the owners of pets. So you see there are opportunities to make money in the pet food business and there are opportunities to become a millionaire business owner in the pet food business.

What you can also do with the example of floor wax is if after years and years of cleaning your house or if after years of having someone clean your house for you, you realize, I'm sure, which floor wax helps give your floor the best shine and which wax enables your floor to keep its best shine even after having people stampeding across your floor on a daily basis. You can take that information and use that information to become a millionaire business owner. You could even take it a step ahead and look at the ingredients of that floor wax and develop for yourself a wax-cleaning solution that would help homeowners and commercial property owners have the best results when they clean their floors. Many millionaire business owners became millionaire business owners by being involved in businesses that were extremely simple and satisfied a very, very basic need such as having clean floors or such as having healthy pets.

Millionaire business owners always know that in order for them to be able to find opportunities in the market, they're going to have to have a high level of information or a high level of exposure in that market. They know that in order for them to recognize opportunities to make money, they're going to have to be involved in the market to a level where they know what it is that the market needs to be improved and what it is that people are looking for in that market which it lacks in providing to customers in order to have a higher level of customer satisfaction. The millionaire business owner will go ahead since he or she is involved in that market and knows what it is that they need to deliver to the marketplace in order for the marketplace to become more satisfied.

Of course, as the expression goes, if you build a better mousetrap, you'll soon have the world knocking at your door. It's not always enough to build a better mousetrap; you'll of course have to let people know that you have that better mousetrap. If you have a high level of expertise in the field or a high level of education in the field, you'll know when the world wants a better mousetrap and what it takes to build a better mousetrap. So, as you can see, from becoming an expert in your field or by having exposure to other experts in the field, you'll be able to become enough of an expert to always be able to anticipate the needs of your market. You'll be able to know how to satisfy those needs. It's not enough to know what your market is looking for as it is not enough even to know how to satisfy what your market is looking for, but you'll need to be able to be an expert in your field to know how you can go ahead to satisfy the market that you're going to be serving.

People who end up becoming millionaire business owners have such a high level of expertise in the market that they're working in that they're always able to introduce new products or services that enable them to make money because they're continuously able to draw new customers and to draw more business from their existing customers because they're always introducing into the marketplace products or services that are needed. If you say to yourself that you don't want to spend the time becoming an expert in the field and/or that you don't know any experts in the field in which you're considering becoming involved or in the field that you enjoy, then therefore you want to become involved in that field, what I would say to you is not to give up but what I would tell you is that you need to very closely examine in what it is that you could be considered an expert. It doesn't have to be anything fancy or sophisticated. It could be something that you do on a daily basis. It could be something that's part of a mundane routine. It really doesn't matter what it is, as long as it meets the criteria of allowing you to become an expert in the field, or allowing you to have a very high level of information or education in the field. Then you're going to be able to succeed in that field.

In order for you to become successful in business, in order to have a good chance of attaining a millionaire business owner status, you're going to have to recognize what it is that you know and what it is that you're very comfortable doing. The two criteria that we have mentioned so far is that first, you have to truly enjoy what it is that you do, and that two, you have to become an expert in what it is that you do, meaning that you have to have a high level of knowledge in what it is that you're going to do before you start.

What happens is that these two qualifications fit together. If you have a high level of interest in a field because you enjoy it immensely, you're going to gain a significant amount of information and expertise simply because enjoy it. If you start out by not enjoying the business in which you are going to be involved and by not having a high level of expertise in the field, you're going to find it extremely challenging to become successful. Even if become successful in that business, you're not going to have what it takes to persevere and keep looking for the next level to attain success. Those who are able to attain a very high level of success are able to do that because they were involved in a business that met both qualifications. They were involved in a business that they enjoyed, that they liked a lot, and with which they enjoyed being involved because it was in a field that they truly enjoyed or that they had been involved in either as a hobby or something that they enjoyed doing. They became very knowledgeable about it, will always have much information upon which to draw, and they'll be able to know what it is that they need to do in order to succeed in that business.

In order to become a millionaire business owner, you need to make a list of in what it is that you're an expert and what it is that you truly enjoy. Next you'll need to see what items on the list can be combined or fit well together and then you need to be able to find a way to make money in that area in order for you to become successful.

I will show you throughout the book examples of how millionaire business owners were able to discover and develop opportunities to make money within fields that they enjoyed or in which they were an expert. You also need to use your imagination in order to find ways to meet that criterion so that you can become extremely successful and so that you can have the opportunity to become a millionaire business owner.

Now let me leave you with one last thought. There is always an opportunity to make money and there's always an opportunity to make a lot of money as long as you have the right motivation to keep pushing you through both good and bad times. Think about how much easier it would be to push yourself in a business when you're doing something that you truly enjoy and that you truly understand.

3

Before starting a business, there is a key ingredient which will be the element that will enable a successful business to truly become successful and to rise above its competition and to make a big impact in the marketplace. Millionaire business owners know what this is, they know this ingredient. Not only do they know this ingredient, they make sure that it's a component of every area of their life. You'll notice that before they're involved in any facet of their life, whether it's business or social, they will always make sure to have this ingredient in their menu, so to speak. They will always make sure that they always follow this principle. This is what enables them to find new opportunities and to be able to become successful with those opportunities, whether they're social or financial.

You see, one of the key factors that many people overlook is that successful business owners always have a very high and level of grasp in the area of business into which they're going. That high level of information that they have doesn't always come because you're an expert in the area. Even if they're an expert in the area, they make sure to have a lot of information that doesn't naturally come to a person by being well-versed in a specific field. What they do is to make sure and do considerable research into any business that they are going to open. They spend countless hours, sometimes weeks if not months, researching a business before they open that business.

When we see these millionaire business owners opening up their businesses and we see them attain a very high level of success, sometimes in a very quick time in which we see their businesses developing very rapidly, we think that their business is developing very rapidly only because they're such great business owners or because they're such successful business people. The truth is that the reason that they're able to grow their business at a very rapid pace from the time that they open up the front doors is because they have already done a lot of research that enables them to know what services and products they need to provide, at what prices they need to provide those products and services, and what types of characteristics need to be delivered by the products and services that they have in order to match up within the area.

When they go ahead and do all of the research and they're able to successfully select what it is that will work in that area, then they already have a huge advantage over the competition. What they're doing is just saying to themselves, in order for my product or service to be able to be successful, I need to know the following:

What people will be willing to pay for it?

What it is that people are willing to pay for?

What mode or fashion do they want to receive that product or service?

If I am able to deliver my product or service in that proper mode or fashion, then that market will want the product or service and I'll experience a high level of demand for the product or service that I offer and will be able to make a lot of money with it. If you're offering a product or service I the new market or any market for that matter, you want to make sure that you have a very high level understanding of the market to which you're going to be offering.

In order to have that high degree of understanding of the market to which you are going to be offering, you need to be able to do a lot of research. So what separates extremely successful business owners that I like to call millionaire business owners from other successful business owners or from any business owners for that matter is that they make sure to do all their research.

You need to spend a lot of time speaking to people, contacting trade groups, contacting the Chamber of Commerce, contacting local government representatives, even contacting other businesses that are already operating in that area. You'd be surprised at how many businesses that you might consider to be a competitor of yours that might still be willing to help you. You see, most people do want to help other people and as long as they don't feel that you're an immediate competition to them, they're going to be very open with you. They're going to share information with you. For instance, if you're opening up a discount store next to a clothing store, as long as you're not selling clothing in your discount store, the owner of the clothing store will be willing to share a lot of her information with you.

Part of doing your research is speaking to businesses in the location where you're planning on opening up. If you're opening a business to business where you're selling to the corporate level or you're selling to other businesses, the location where you open up might not be that important. In that situation, you'll want to speak to businesses that currently sell to the corporate community or that sell to other businesses so that you can know what are the standard procedures that a business must take when its involved in the business to business marketplace.

You see, a millionaire business owner is always doing the research. They don't just do research before they open up a business, but they're always doing research on a consistent basis. As situations change and new opportunities arise, they're always making sure that they stay in the loops and that they're knowledgeable and that they know how to respond. The way that they stay in the loop is by always having a network of people with whom they constantly talk and with whom they share ideas.

One thing that millionaire business owners know is that in order to be able to gain a lot of information, they also need to be able to give information. By staying involved in the business circles and having an active role in the business community and in the business community in which they're planning on operating, they'll always be able to be a source of information for other people. If you are a source of credible information and concrete information that can help other people succeed in their businesses, then those people are going to want to be able to gain your favor. They're going to want to be able to gain information from you; they're going to also provide you with good solid information.

So the key for any successful business owner is to make sure that you're always in the network, that you're always in the know and that you're always able to have a flow of information. You need to be able to always speak to people and to other businesses and to constantly do your research. Then you're going to have a very good chance of being able to have outpaced the competition and of being able to make money in your business.

The reverse is true if that business owner doesn't always speak to people involved in the business and doesn't keep contacts with people operating in the same marketplace in which he or she is operating. Very soon, they won't be able to keep up to date with changing developments, they will know what the new, hot products or services that the market demands, and they'll find themselves n a situation where their competition will quickly out-maneuver them because their competition will know what products or services are in demand. The competition will start offering those products or services and the business that they are running will not be able to have those same products or services, especially in a timely fashion because it will be too late before they realize that the market now is asking for those products and services.

If you want to make sure at all times that you're able to always stay ahead of your competition, it won't be enough just to speak to businesses operating in the marketplace because those businesses will pretty much know just as much as you know because their ideas and their strategies will be a reflection of what is occurring in the marketplace. If you want to stay a step ahead, you need to actually focus on trade magazines that cover that industry. You need to find out what it is that the experts are saying regarding that industry. If the experts in that industry feel that the marketplace now is going to start shifting to more expensive items, as long as the quality is of a higher caliber, then you need to start carrying higher-quality products, even if they're priced higher or if you find out from the experts that now people prefer that all of their food should be low-fat, then you have to start serving low-fat food to your customers.

The only way that you'll know this before it's too late or before your competitors know it is by staying one step ahead, meaning that you always speak to people who are one level above you. Speak to not just retailers, also speak to wholesalers. If you're a wholesaler, speak to manufacturers. If you're a manufacturer, speak to importers and exporters. Only when you can't, speak actually to consumers who're using your products and services so that you can know their preferences. You want to know are they looking for products or services that serve needs that are financially related, that are service related, and that are quality related. You always need to be on top of things and the best way to do it is to actually be interacting on a daily basis with the people who will be using your products or services.

Millionaire business owners know the importance of playing every role in their organizations so they can always interact with every level of customer that the organization possesses. Sam Walton, the founder of Wal-Mart, while he was alive would visit different Wal-Mart locations and would speak to the customers who frequented his stores. By speaking to the customers who frequented his stores, he immediately knew what products his customers were looking for; he knew if they were happy with the quality of the products that he carried. He also knew if they were happy with the prices that he was charging.

I once went to a gas station in New Jersey that was located a few blocks away from the corporate headquarters for the owner of that that national chain of gas stations. At that gas station, by the way he was dressed and by the way he spoke to the customers, there was one person pumping gas whom you could tell was not an ordinary employee of the gas station. When I got into a conversation with him, I discovered that he was actually an executive at the corporate headquarters, but as a part of his training period, he would have to spend one week pumping gas at a gas station so he could see first hand the interaction between the customer and the gas station and so that he could see the level of satisfaction that the customers had, and also so that he could see whether the customers preferred a certain type of gas, a certain type of a service, and whether they were satisfied with the prices that the gas station was charging.

The only way that this can be done is by actually being involved at the retail level and by being involved with the consumers and the customers of the business. Just like this national gas company sent its executives to its stores for training, which in this case were its gas stations, you'll also need to go ahead and make sure to always stay in touch with the street to find out on a basic level, or the street level, what it is that your customers want, what it is that they're looking for, what it is that they're happy with, with what are they unhappy.

Millionaire business owners know that at all times, whether it's before they open up a business, whether it's while they're running a business, or while they're looking to sell their business, they're always involved with people who run businesses similar to their business. They're speaking to vendors who supply their business, they're speaking to wholesalers, to retailers who are involved in their business, whether they're selling business to business or business to retail, or the consumer to consumer business such as maybe an organization that helps consumers, they're always making sure to always do their research so that they always know the pulse of the market, what products are needed and what products are not needed.

Unfortunately, there are many, many business owners who sometimes stock up on a product or devote themselves towards providing a service which is no longer needed and soon becomes out of style. Those business owners then lose a lot of money because they're now offering a product or a service that is no longer needed or no longer in demand. If you want to make sure that you're able to offer a product or a service which is not in demand and you don't want to find yourself in a situation where you've overstocked yourself with a product or where you hire service providers that are no longer needed and all the money that you've invested is now gone, the way to be able to avoid that type of situation is by always doing your research so you can see to what direction the market is moving. You'll be able to analyze which products and services will be needed.

Millionaire business owners always seem to stay one step ahead of the crowd by knowing what trends are taking place in the marketplace. Then, the proactively respond to those trends and they're able to capitalize on making money by being ready for those trends when they do take place.

To recap some of the best research methods that millionaire business owners use are reading trade journals that cover the industry or by reading general magazines that don't cover the industry, they can be entertainment magazines or magazines that are for the consumer, but while reading those magazines they will be able to pick up on what products or services customers like, what they enjoy, what movies they're seeing, what types of foods they enjoy eating and what kinds of toys with which their children play.

Millionaire business owners also subscribe to more expensive research methods. They sometimes use focus groups. You could assemble your own focus group because a focus group that's provided by a corporation could sometimes cost over ten thousand dollars. Many corporations are in the business of providing focus groups. A focus group is a group of potential customers who might use your product or service and are assembled to be asked questions and shown different products, to see if they have a preference regarding what type of product or service, what prices they're willing to pay, and what characteristics they would like to see in a product or service so that they would be willing to use it, what the product or service could have so that people would use more of it.

Now, you can assemble your own focus group by gathering some of your friends together, by giving them a small incentive, such as a free sample of the product or service. You can gather those friends together or maybe some members of you family or relatives, you could find college students, high school students, maybe some retirees and you could run your own focus group. You can ask them what they think about your product or service, ask them what you can do to improve your product or service, and ask them what price they'd be willing to pay for that product or service.

When I ran a few web sites which sold e-books, I would have people examining my e-books, reading the e-books, telling me whether they thought I was providing a decent amount of information, if they felt that I needed to provide more information, if I needed to update the e-book, or if I needed to provide a higher level of detailed information. I would also ask them about the price and find out not only what price they thought was a fair price, but also what was the highest price that they would be willing to pay for one of my e-books. You see sometimes, people undersell their product or service by charging too little for what they are selling.

For instance, I sold one of my e-books for $29.00, but I soon discovered that I could sell that same e-book for as much as $97.00. I discovered that by speaking to people and also by trial and error. Millionaire business owners know that in order for them to make money, it's not always a matter of selling volume, but it's also sometimes a matter of charging a high enough price for the product that when they do sell their products or services, they can produce a high level of revenue that will help them reach millionaire status.

One of the best sources of research is by actually walking into a mall or walking into a store, walking into a restaurant or into a company, and seeing what products or services they offer, which products or services are used the most, and what prices for which these products and services are being offered. That way you can make your own decisions and decide whether you're charging too little or too much, whether the product or service you're selling is of high quality, if the service you're offering is a service that is in demand and whether it will continue to be in demand.

You see, there are many ways to do research. The most important thing is that you're always doing research and that you always remember that even when you're research seems unnecessary that millionaire business owners attribute a large amount of their success to the research that they have done and that they continue doing on a consistent basis.

4

Millionaire business owners know that in order for them to be successful in business they're going to need to have the resources that are derived from the ability of people to network together and people to act together in the interest of another individual or another group or thing. In this situation, millionaire business owners know that in order for them to be very successful in their businesses they're going to need to draw upon not just the knowledge and expertise of an expert in the field or another business person in the field, or even on their own expertise or own level of knowledge and access to information, but rather that they're going to need to be able to draw upon the resources and information that people from a diverse area will be able to provide them

You see, successful entrepreneurs and successful business owners know one thing and that is that you can't be an expert in everything and that you don't always need to be an expert in everything in order to succeed, but you do need to have access to information in every area in which your business will be involved and in every area which will apply to your business. They way that you do that, the way that you ensure that you always have access to the information that you need and that you always have access to experts who can help you along with your business is by being able to draw upon the resources from those people. Now, how do you ensure that you'll always have someone to ask and that you'll always have someone to whom you can talk when you need to discuss a vital issue concerning your business? The way that you do that is to make sure that you have a relationship with someone, with an individual, a company, a nonprofit organization, or a government agency that can supply you that information on a practical level.

Millionaire business owners know that in order for them to succeed in their business, they are going to need to have what is called a board of directors. A board of directors is an entity which you can set up on your own. It's the same type of an entity that major public corporations have for which they go ahead and invite certain people having a certain amount of expertise in their fields, people who are very well-respected by the public and who have good relationships with the public or private sector, to sit on their board of directors. Those people provide guidance and advice to the company while it pursues its business strategies.

Millionaire business owners like to have a board of directors because it always ensures that they'll always have somebody to ask for information and they'll always be able to have their questions answered as needed. The board of directors establishes a group of individuals who will always be able to provide you with a good amount of information that you'll need in the course of your business.

In order for you to have a board of directors, you don't have to have people like Henry Kissinger on your board, which of course wouldn't hurt. If you're a small business owner or an entrepreneur who is just starting out, you're probably not going to have those types of contacts. If you do have those types of contacts, then I strongly urge you to get those people to be on your board of directors. If you're like the rest of us when you're first starting out at the beginning stages of your business, then you need to try to emulate as closely as possible the board of directors that millionaire business owners use.

Millionaire business owners have a board of directors consisting of their attorney, their accountant, their financial adviser, and other people who can play an important role in the guidance of their business. If you have a business that will be set up to sell socks to discount stores such as I do, what you would want to do is organize a board of directors consisting of people who have an expertise in the retail business, the wholesale business, and specifically in the sock business.

Now, this board of directors could be formal, in which you would let those people know their role, you ask them to join your board of directors, and you set up specific times where you will all meet as a group or you can meet one-on-one with them. You can also set up this board of directors on an informal basis. On an informal basis, the board of directors would be available to answer specific types of questions. The input of these key people would correspond to different aspects of your business.

For instance with my business, I don't just wholesale socks, I wholesale a variety of merchandise to discount stores, to 99-cents stores, to flea market vendors, and to small boutiques. My informal board of directors consists of these people, an accountant, an attorney, a financial adviser, and it also consists of people who have an active role in the retail and wholesale business. I have people to whom I can speak and upon whose years of expertise and being involved in the challenging wholesale or retail business I can draw and of whom I can ask questions such as "What are the best products to sell to stores? What products do stores need at different times of the year? Which stores will be the best customers for the types of products that I am looking to sell? What is the best way to approach a new store? What is the best way to market myself? What is the best way to keep records for my business? What is the best way to invest my money in the business? What type of contract do I need to construct or when is a contract necessary? What kind of arrangement can I set up with a consultant so that the consultant is not considered an employee? What kind of agreement do I need to prepare between a consultant and me?"

You see, every business has features that are of a legal nature, a financial nature, a practical nature, such as obtaining merchandise, selling merchandise, hiring employees, laying off employees, expanding the business, looking for a location, reviewing a lease, or entering into a lease. Whatever type of business you are involved in, I can assure you that you will be able to benefit if you have people from whom you can always ask advice, with whom you can always meet, and for whom you can pick up the telephone and call to set up a time to meet with them. I strongly suggest that you always use your board of directors.

If you realize that public companies, by their very nature, and because they became public companies, are usually more successful than private companies. While you can always find examples that will go against this rule, it is safe to say that for the most part, large corporations, such as the ones that are listed in the NYSE make more money and have a larger volume of business than small, modest shop operations. One thing you'll notice about large corporations is that they all have a board of directors. There are many private corporations and private businesses that even though they're not listed in the NYSE, they still have a board of directors because they realize that there is nothing better than being able to simply pick up the phone and set up a meeting with one of the members of their board of directors to discuss any question that may arise.

In one of my business venture, I needed to set up a catalog. Since I had an ongoing relationship with an individual who is now retired, but was involved in the wholesale business for twenty-five years, I was able to call him. Because this individual is very generous, both with his time and his patience, he was able to give me guidance on how to set up a catalog, how to develop a mailing list, and how to mail it. He went out of his way to find an old catalog that he had and give it to me so that I could use it to formulate my own catalog. This way, I would not have to start from scratch, but would be able to base my catalog on the work of a professional who was involved for twenty-five years in the same type of business in which I was involved. So see, there are many other benefits of having a board of directors.

Let's say you need to start an advertising campaign and you're trying to decide in which publication you need to advertise. Should you use the newspaper, should you use a magazine, should you use direct mail and mail out all your offerings to your potential customers? If you have access to an individual who is involved in your business, you can ask that individual for his or her opinion regarding each advertising medium and then ask which advertising medium he or she most prefers, how he or she advertised in those mediums, and what he or she suggests for you.

Sometimes you also want to have people on your board of directors who might not have been actively involved in the same business as you but who have a lot of business expertise. For example if you're thinking about opening a pet grooming salon, now you might not need someone who has experience in the engraving business, but what someone in the engraving business might be able to provide for you is advice in such areas as how to select the best location because both an engraver and the owner of a pet grooming salon both need to find a location from which they can work. They can give you advice about how to go about negotiating a price with the landlord for the rent on the establishment, how to negotiate a lease, what to look out for, what to avoid in a lease, how to contact suppliers, and how to find suppliers. Now he can't tell you from where you'll be able to find suppliers of pet grooming supplies, but he can tell you when you do find the supplier how he or she went about finding suppliers. You can then use that information to find suppliers on your own.

You see there are many levels of advice which you can receive. Sometimes you want to receive specific business advice and sometimes you want to receive general business advice. Sometimes you'll want to also have access to what I would call "common sense" advice. You might want to have a teacher on your board of directors since a teacher is a great person to be able to ask questions of when it comes to business. The reason a teacher is a great person with whom to discuss your business is because a teacher is actively involved with people. A teacher knows what motivates people and what scares people. A teacher knows how to encourage and how to discourage. A teacher has very good social skills, research skills, and a teacher has also had to develop the ability to communicate new thoughts and to communicate old ideas in new, dynamic and exciting ways to an audience that is not always interested in what the teacher has to say. I'm sure you and I have both been exposed to a teacher who had a great ability to teach, to get his class excited, to get his class invigorated to go over a subject that neither you nor I really like, but once we both started hearing what this teacher had to say, we both were excited and said not only does this subject make sense, but I am more interested in finding out more about it. So a teacher can also help you by giving you business guidance such as telling which way is the best way to explain your business to prospects and what about your business to highlight. A teacher can tell you what it is about your business that needs more explanation; a teacher can help you with grammatical issues, with putting together a catalog to use in your direct mail campaign by supplying you with good English words that will help convey your message in a very clear, concise way. See a teacher can do a lot for you.

A teacher is someone who by nature is teaching and that is what you're doing to your prospects. When you have a customer, you want to convert that potential customer into a buying customer. You want to develop a long-term relationship, so you're going to need to find out how to highlight the benefits of your products or services. You need to know how to market your business, its products or services to prospective customers who might not be that interested in what you're offering or that might not even realize their need for what you're offering. You'll need to be able to proceed in the best way to market what you're offering and explain to people why they need what you're offering.

See, there are two ways to sell, one of which is selling something people clearly need and clearly want. That's a much easier type of sale. If you have a restaurant that serves hamburgers and hotdogs, then that's going to be a very easy sale. Everybody likes hamburgers and hotdogs. The challenge with that business is that there's going to be an immense amount of competition since everybody knows how easy it is to sell hotdogs and hamburgers, there are going to be a lot of establishments devoted specifically towards that type of food. Now a product in the food category or in the restaurant industry that people might not realize that they need could be a restaurant that specifically is devoted towards serving organically grown vegetables. That type of a restaurant will have a hard time initially finding customers because people might not be interested in eating organically grown vegetables and they might not even be aware of the benefits of eating organically grown vegetables. Your role now is going to be to get people excited about organic vegetables and also to tell them and to show them that there is a reason why they should want to eat what you have to offer. A teacher can help you by giving you a clear method to illustrate the benefits of the vegetables that you'll be serving in a way that people will become interested in wanting to eat them because they'll know why they need to eat them and will understand the benefits of eating those vegetables.

Remember, the more exciting you make your products or services, the more money you'll be able to make when you do sell those products or services. Now why would you want to open up an organic vegetable restaurant? The reason is that anytime you open up a restaurant or a business you offer a product or service that has no competition or very little competition and you're able to draw customers to your business, you'll be able to make a lot of money because you're not going to be faced with any competition and your customers will not be faced with too many choices. If they're interested in what it is that you're offering, they'll find that you're one of the only resources available for your products or services.

Now there are many more ideas that you might be able to obtain when you have a good board of directors. If you're trying to decide what type of business you want to go into, you'll find that it might make sense to have either a formal or an informal arrangement with various people whom you feel have a lot of life experience. These are people with whom you can discuss things who can supply you with good advice, will provide you with effective strategy, will offer you positive encouragement and motivate you along the way, and at the same time have a realistic outlook that will help keep you in check. By keeping you in check I mean that they have ideas that are grounded and that when you have an idea that is not the best idea in the world, and we all have to admit that it happens to the best of us when we sometimes have an idea that we feel will help us make money when in reality, that idea is not so well thought out and will not work in the real world. This means that we all need people who will remind us when ideas won't work just as much we need their encouragement when we have good ideas.

We also need people who are able to come up with ideas on their own. We want to have people who are knowledgeable enough in their areas to be able to see an opportunity when it arises. Our board of directors will need to consist of professionals who are self-employed, who are blue-collar workers, and who, regardless of who they are, they are hard workers. As long as they're actively involved in their profession, whether they're painters, car mechanics, carpenters, plumbers, attorneys, nurses, doctors, government workers, just as long as they're involved in what it is that they're doing, they'll be able to see opportunities to make money in their fields. Many people, since they're not interested in being in business, will be very happy to share their ideas with you. If they spot a good opportunity to make money, they'll be happy to share that idea with you.

Sometimes even people who are in business for themselves are so overwhelmed and tied up with the business that they're running, that when they see an opportunity to make money they just will not have the time to pursue that opportunity. They sometimes may not have the resources even if they do have the time. Let's say the owner of a business is devoting all of his money into running his business, which in this case let's say is a landscaping business. As he makes his rounds, he notices that the houses in a certain area don't have clear number signs on the property, meaning that when you drive by that property it is very hard to see the number which is part of the address for each house. That landscaper might not have the time or the money to be able to purchase various plastic or wooden numbers to sell to the owners of these homes. He instead might be willing to pass that idea along to you so that you can go ahead and develop a business where you fashion nice, fancy lettering which you can go ahead and sell to homeowners. For an extra service fee, you can even place the letters on the homes so that those homes have a more visible address sign. You see there is a very big problem sometimes for police, EMT workers, and firemen, who upon trying to respond to a call for help or upon seeing or hearing a signal for help, they aren't able to exactly locate a house because the address isn't visible. Then they lose a lot of crucial time in responding to that emergency. So there is a very big demand, and I know of people who make money by supplying very clear address signs for homes. This way if there's an emergency, the emergency personnel can quickly see the address and can quickly respond to the emergency.

A landscaper could also be a great source of information because he could tell you if homes within a certain area needed to be painted or if they needed better security protection. He could tell you if there are other products or services that those homeowners could use. The same could apply to someone who has an alterations business or someone who has a dry cleaning store. He sees that most of his customers only own one suit. He might alert you to the fact that the area could use a source of cheap suits. In other words, he could say "My customers keep on having their suits dry cleaned. They really need their suits. They need to have fancy shirts, they need fancy pants, but it's an economically depressed area and the people here just can't afford to pay the prices of the local department store." That dry cleaner might give you an idea to open up a store selling good quality, affordable suits that have fancy pants and fancy shirts.

When you have a board of directors, you'll have a group of people from whom you can constantly receive ideas, with whom you can discuss your ideas, and discuss any legal or tax issues that arise. This way you'll be able to overcome the challenges people find in businesses when they don't have anyone with whom they can talk. On the positive side, one of the best benefits that you'll have is that you'll be able to quickly make a decision. Anytime a new problem or a new challenge arises you'll have people you can quickly contact to obtain the information you need. millionaire business owners know that in order for them to succeed in their business, they always need to have a set of individuals or either a group of people which we will call a board of directors with whom they can have a formal or informal relationship where they can obtain all of the answers for their questions. They will be able to obtain leads, advice, and opportunities that they would not have found on their own.

5

What do you think enables an entrepreneur to truly succeed in business? Is it in having a high level of intelligence, is it in having a high level of expertise, is it in having a lot of luck, is it being exposed to a good opportunity? Millionaire business owners attribute much of their success to not luck, not even having the right opportunity, not even always to working hard. While they do say that all of those components are important in order for them to succeed, one of the more prevailing ideas that millionaire business owners have, and one of the strategies that they fully utilize and to which they attribute their success is that they always work in teams as opposed to working alone.

You see, why the term "self-employed" denotes a person who works by himself or herself, it is really misinterpreted to mean an individual who is working by themselves. In order to succeed in life, you need to look at successful examples of organizations or entities that succeed. If you think about a family, and a family is the most basic unit in our world which has different levels of success and also you can measure what families accomplish and in which directions they go. Families are stronger and are on average, more financially stable than individuals. The reason is because a family is able to draw upon the resources of each other, it's able to draw upon the expertise of each other, it's presented opportunities by different members of the family, and it receives moral and physical support from the different members of the family. An individual has to draw upon his or her own resources, his or her own expertise, his or her own physical ability, his own motivational ability, his or her own moral support, and has to find opportunities on his or her own. On the other hand, a family unit allows the brother to be able to give the sister a job opportunity. If he sees a job available in his area, he can let his sister know about the opportunity. A father can tell his son about a great school or a great course of which he has heard. A daughter can tell her mother about a great store to do her shopping. All those are very basic examples, but those examples take place in any type of an organization in any type of a setting where there are different individuals cooperating together or working together.

Millionaire business owners always try to set up their businesses so that there is teamwork involved. Even when they don't have employees working for them, they delegate work whenever it is possible. millionaire business owners know that in order for them to succeed they will not be able to do everything on their own, so when they have an opportunity and when it is feasible, they send out work to other individuals. For example, let's say a millionaire business owner needed to purchase a new computer. Once he purchased that computer he would need to find a way to bring that computer to his office, set up the computer, load the software, and learn how to use the new computer. Those activities could take that millionaire business owner anywhere from three to five days. It would take him a day to do the shopping, another day or two to set up the computer and install the software, and maybe another day or so of learning how to use the computer and the software, he would be on his feet and ready to go.

A millionaire business owner knows that even though he might have to spend more money at the beginning, that by spending money initially will enable him to move farther ahead in his business and that to succeed in his business, it is worth it. So a millionaire business owner would actually contact someone in the computer industry, someone who is in the business of selling computers and ask that individual to sell him a computer, deliver the computer, set up the computer, install the software, and show him how to use the computer.

A millionaire business owner for example who wants the right sales copy for an offering he will be sending out to his customers will contact a professional who has experience in writing ad copy. The millionaire business owner knows that while he or she can learn how to write ad copy, it will take them countless trial and error runs until they're able to formulate a great letter to send out to their customers, but if they use a professional, they'll have a great letter which is ready to be used right away. millionaire business owners know that for example, if there business involves a lot of packing, such as my business involves, they're much better delegating the packing work to someone else so that they can devote their focus and their energies towards other areas of business. The millionaire business owner would rather take some money out of his profits to pay someone to the boxes, to take the boxes to the post office, to have the boxes readied for UPS, to take them to the UPS center, and to organize all the merchandise that needs to be sent out to customers. The millionaire business owner would rather pay for all the above if it means that he or she would have more time to devote themselves towards making more money in other areas.

Let's look at an example. The millionaire business owner receives an order from a small discount store chain out in the Midwest. This discount store chain wants to order 500 dozen sweaters, so they're expecting now to get 6000 sweaters, and they specifiy that they would like 20% of them in red, 20% of them in blue, 10% of them in white, and the rest of them in gray. Now the millionaire business owner has two options. He or she knows that on this deal they'll be making $2000.00 after all expenses. Now $2000.00 is a lot of money, especially when it's not the only deal on which you're working. If you have three or four of those types of sales per month, that money starts adding up very quickly.

The two options available to the millionaire business owner are that he can either spend the time assembling the order, going through all of his inventory, selecting the sweaters, counting the sweaters to make sure that he is putting in the right numbers of sweaters by colors, by size, and by style, because of course they won't just request different colors, they'll request different sizes, they'll want to have small, medium, large, extra-large, they might want to have 2XL, they might want to have certain sweaters with designs or certain sweaters without designs. This millionaire business owner can now spend a day or two days assembling this order. He can spend maybe three or four hours on one day and send out the order and keep that entire $2000.00 of profit or the millionaire business owner can go ahead and pay someone $50.00 or $100.00 to put together that order and meanwhile work the phones to find another customer to place a similar order.

Now let's say he is able to find someone to assemble the order and to send out the order and they need two days to work on the order and that he had to hire two people to assemble the order, to pack the order, and to send out the order. The millionaire business owner spent $200.00 on the expense of having someone setting up the order and sending it, so now his profit isn't $2000.000, it's actually only $1800.00. Two hundred dollars might be a lot to a millionaire business owner, but it means a lot to you and me when we're first starting out in business. We might be very tempted to want to save that money and do the packing ourselves so that we can save that profit; however, if that millionaire business owner was able to spend that day or two days that it took packing the order working the phones contacting other potential customers, pulling previous customers, and finding another customer who bought $1000 worth of merchandise, giving him a $400 profit, then his profit is actually $200 because out of the $400 you could say that $200 went to cover the expense of having to set up the order and the other $200 is his profit.

Now let's look at the example this way. There are three orders that need to go out to customers. Every order will give you a $2000 profit.

The three orders were not all placed at the same time. On Monday you had one order for $2000 worth of merchandise and you said "Should I send out this order by myself or should I pay someone $200 to pack the order so I can devote myself to looking for other business?" What you do is go ahead and pay someone $200 to send out that first order and meanwhile you go ahead and are able to make another sale which gives you a $2000 profit. For that order you'll also have to pay someone $200 to set it up so that your time is freed up to look for another order. On your third order you make another $2000 profit, so your total gross profit is $6000, minus the $600 you paid out to have your orders assembled and sent out to your customers. Now your actual net profit is not $6000 but $5400. Even though $5400 isn't a lot of money to make in business, it's definitely a good amount of money to make, you might be a little upset that you had to give up that $600 from your profits, but look at it this way. If you had spent your entire first day when you received that first order packing up that order and sending out that order, you never would have had the time to solicit the second order, and with the second order, you also had spent all the time packing or processing that order yourself, you never would have had the time to find the customer to order the third order from you. Really, in effect if you had done all of the packing yourself, your profit would have probably have been only the first $2000. You would not have had the time or the opportunity to find the two other customers who placed the two additional orders from you.

This is the reason millionaire business owners like using fulfillment centers. A fulfillment center is a business that is in the business processing orders, taking orders on the phone, packing your orders, assembling your orders, sending them out to the customers, keeping track of your orders, and even corresponding with the customer to make sure that the customer was happy with the product or service that they received. A fulfillment center can also do some of the prospecting. There are telemarketing organizations that will go ahead and make phone calls for you. You can supply a list of prospects to a telemarketing center which will charge you between $15-$20 an hour to call the people on the list and ask them if they would like to try your product or service. Many companies such as BellAtlantic, the Wall Street Journal, the New York Times, the New York Philharmonic, VISA, and Mastercard use telemarketing services to call potential customers and to find out if those customers would be interested in hearing more about their products or services that they're offering. Many telemarketing centers will actually try to sell the product while others will only formulate the lead for you, meaning they'll call and once they find out that prospect is interested in hearing more about your product or service they will then pass on that information to you. The reason you might want to use a telemarketing service that will not actually do the entire sale for you is because you feel that you might have more experience and will have the ability to better convey the benefits of your product or service. If you have a telemarketing service which does all of the selling for you they might do a bad job in actually selling which could cause you to miss out on a lot of opportunities to make money when you could have been instead selling that product or service. A good telemarketing center will have people who are experienced in what you're offering, but there's never a better replacement for the owner of the business who has the most at stake. Also, by nature the owner of that business who is actively involved in that business will have better answers to the questions that prospects might ask.

Millionaire business owners know that while they always want to out place as much work as possible, they want to be able to delegate as many tasks as they can, they also want to make sure not to have any barriers between themselves and the customers. A telemarketer calling a potential customer and advising the potential customer about her product or service is great, it's only great when that telemarketer now will turn around and pass that lead on to you.

When I was an intern in college, I worked for a very successful financial planner who had me calling prospects and letting them know of the services that he offered. When I spoke with an individual who was interested in the product or service being offered, whether it was the offering of a stock, a bond, or simply a financial planning service such as retirement planning, or setting up a college education plan, when that individual was interested in hearing more, I would jot down that person's name and phone number and would let them know that the financial planner would be contacting them soon. Then I would walk into the office of the financial planner and give him the lead and he would go ahead and call and try to close the sale.

A millionaire business owner knows that to fully succeed in business they need to be the ones to either actually make the sale or to be involved in the sale. If you have a telemarketing outfit that is calling prospects for you and because they have a lot of experience in the field in which you're involved, so you let them actually do the sale, you want to make sure to be the only one to call your customer as soon as they use your product or service so you can find out how they're doing. You can see that they're enjoying the product or service and if they have any qualms about it before they return that product or before they cancel the usage of your services. You want to have the opportunity to speak to them and to discuss with them any issues that might arise. Millionaire business owners always stay involved in every aspect of the customer relationship because they know of the benefits that it will provide for them in the long run.

Now, there are firm believers in using teamwork. For instance, there are many other areas of business which while they might be able to master and which might be very simple for them to do. If the owner of a business knows that he or she needs to keep very careful track of the expenses of the business, of the revenues of the business, of the customers of the customers that the business has, they might want to deal with a bookkeeper. A bookkeeper is someone who simply will keep a record of the expenses of the business, the sales of the business, the profits of the business, with whom the business is dealing, who are the suppliers are, and who are the customers. An owner of a business might know that he or she can actually do the same thing on their own and that they really don't need this bookkeeper, but a millionaire business owner realizes that he or she would rather not be involved with the mundane activities of a business such as bookkeeping when they could actually be involved in more needed areas of the business such as selling the product, looking for suppliers of the product, perfecting the product, offering a better service, and looking for more business opportunities with which to make money for the business. If they instead devote themselves to more simple things such as organizational activity, such as bookkeeping activities, and such as accounting issues that really are more clerical in nature than business in nature, then the owner of that business would rather delegate that activity or delegate that business to someone else. So millionaire business owners always decide what will give them the most benefit from their business, what effort and energy will result in the highest level of profit. Even though paying a bookkeeper will cost an extra amount of money and there is an extra expense associated with that bookkeeping activity, they know that in the long run they'll be able to free up more time to devote themselves to actually making money with the business. And another thing that takes place is that the individual who provides the bookkeeping service is actually an expert in providing bookkeeping services and therefore, will be able to provide a much better service to the owner of the business than the millionaire business owner can provide himself. You see a millionaire business owner is not a bookkeeper by nature. He or she does not know all the best ways to keep track of expenses, to keep track of the revenue, and to keep track of sales. A millionaire business owner has not been exposed to that area and it might bore him. If it bores him then he'll find himself making mistakes and not keeping accurate records; therefore, a millionaire business owner would rather find someone who is proficient in that area. Then this way, not only will the service be offered at a very professional level, but the service will always be available and the actual service itself will be done. You or I might become lazy when we do bookkeeping, we might become lazy when we keep track of our records because we might to say to ourselves "You know what, I'll do that tomorrow, I'll write down this customer's name later on in the day, I'll look for that number later, you know I don't really need this number now, it's not so important." But a bookkeeper, since he or she knows that it's their obligation to keep records for the business and they're being paid for it, will not let their laziness interfere. It's not that a business owner is lazy because business owners are the hardest working people that I know, but millionaire business owners know that they are simply not interested in that activity and would rather find someone else who will because they are paid make sure that the activity is full done. Once again, millionaire business owners know that in order to attain millionaire status and in order to have an extremely successful business with a high level of revenue and profitability, they need to devote themselves specifically to the process of making money with their businesses.

6

Millionaire business owners know who is a true source of success for their business. While most business owners when asked who will actually make them rich in their business, they are quick to answer that their customers are the ones who help their businesses grow. Very few of them realize that actually the most important people for any business are the employees of the business. If the owner of the business is the only employee or whether the business has 100 employees, those employees are the ones who will truly direct the direction of the business and will truly mold the success of the business. See while the customer is great and the customer is essential because the customer is the one that actually puts money into your pockets, it is an employee who the one who is finding those customers, who is servicing those customers, and who is ensuring that those customers pay. Many businesses make a mistake when they deal with the customer by actually always siding with the customer if a customer complains and a customer is upset and a dispute comes out in the open and it puts the employee in an embarrassing situation, they will still rush to defend the customer even though the customer might be embarrassing the employee. That's a big mistake because remember, those customers come and go, they might buy from you today or they might not buy from you today. While the customer is surely important and all customers should be treated very honestly and fairly, your employee needs to be treated even better. Your employee is the one who has the most loyalty to you. You can say from a practical point that your employee is getting a paycheck from you and therefore, your employee is going to want what is best for you and will always have the business' interest in mind or you can say from a nicer point of view that an employee has developed a relationship with his employer and wants to help out his employer to see the business succeed. Regardless of which outlook you take, in both situations you see a crucial role that your employee plays. An employee who is satisfied with his job will make up for any lost customers.

Say for example that you have a sales person who is servicing a beverage route. His job is to go out and look for more stores and when he finds those stores he has to make deliveries of cases of beverages. One time by mistake, or maybe even because he got lazy and didn't take his time counting the number of beverages he was supposed to deliver, the employee only delivers two and a half cases instead of a full three cases. The store gets extremely upset and calls you up and tells you that this sales person told them that he was going to deliver three cases, but this sales person is so incompetent that he only delivered two and a half cases. After apologizing to the customer and telling the customer that you're going to make up for it, that he shouldn't be worried, that you're going to immediately send out the sales person with another half a case so that they should have exactly what they ordered, at that point you have two options. You've already made good with the customer, you've told the customer that you're going to resolve the situation, now you can either get upset at your sales person and reprimand him or you could discuss the situation with him and see how you could ensure that it doesn't happen again. You see if you get upset at the sales person, then the sales person might quit and you won't have anyone to service those accounts or to look for new accounts in that area. If you're nice to the sales person and you explain to him what happened the sales person will appreciate the way you treated him and he'll make sure the next time that he delivers the right amount of beverages to each location. And if you do lose that account because of the sales person, I still would not recommend your firing that sales person because if you show that sales person how you're still willing to give him the chance even though due to his mistake or due to his oversight he lost a customer for you, since he feels appreciated and realizes that you have a good relationship, he will go out of his way not only to make up the business by bringing you a new customer, he might actually out of appreciation for being able to keep his job look for a few more customers to add on to your business. Then at the end of the day, you will benefit. Millionaire business owners realize that employees are always at the forefront of their businesses.

Employees are the ones who deal on a daily basis with customers, employees are the ones who assemble and process your orders, employees are the ones who answer the phones, employees are the ones who do the deliveries, and employees are the ones who support the administrative needs of the business. They know that if the employees are not happy and the employees are not motivated, they'll be in the situation where they'll be in an army of soldiers who have lost the conviction or who have lost the desire to fight. If you have an organization in which all of the employees are treated extremely well, you're nice to the employees, you're supportive of them, and you discuss things with them instead of rushing to reprimand them, then you will have an organization that is similar to an army whose soldiers are not only excited about the battle, who are not only ready to battle, but will always proactively think of better ways to persevere in the battle.

You see an employee is a person after all who has his or her own needs, the employee has his or her own interests, and the employee also has a sense of pride that has to be well-respected. If you can find a balance where an employee is satisfied and feels good about his job and at the same time knows what he or she needs to do, you will have a good team of employees to help you with your business. Millionaire business owners know that you always need to have a balance between keeping your customers happy but at the same time making sure your employees feel valuable and that they never become the scapegoat for any business mistakes that you might make or even that they might make. Let's say that some employees fouled up an order, didn't deliver something on time, didn't process an order correctly, or didn't do their administrative duties the way you wanted them to do them. If you simply fire those employees or reprimand those employees or you lose those employees because you give them a hard time and they quit, you'll have a hard time replacing those employees, and even if you are able to replace those employees in a timely manner, you'll have to retrain those new employees which is a costly and time-laden venture. Instead if you keep your employees on board and there is a low turnover rate at your company, you'll be able to have the satisfaction from having employees know what it is that they need to do and who constantly are involved in the business and who do not need constant training such as new employees would need. Remember, millionaire business owners know that their employees are the heart of their business and they know that if they have good, satisfied employees who are compensated well that their business will also be able to perform well.

Compensation is very important. The compensation that you extend to your employees will encourage them in the business. It will also discourage them from considering employment outside or even starting their own business in the same type of business that you're operating. There are many scenarios in which employees, after learning a business leave that business and start their own business in the same field. Not always because they want to make more money, but sometimes simply because they weren't being treated well in the business in which they were working and instead of looking for another employer they decided to start their own business.

My grandfather, who ran a bakery for over thirty years, knew that it was always very important to keep his employees well compensated and well satisfied. This way they showed up to work early, they stayed long hours, they put an extra effort into their work, and sometimes were proactive and came up with new recipes for cookies, designed nice cakes, and came up with new ideas about how to make the customers happier that my grandfather might not have come up with on his own.

If those employees were not satisfied and they were not happy, they never would have put in the extra amount of effort and there would have been a high turnover rate. Every time you're forced to hire a new employee, you have to go through the training process again, so compensating your employees is very important. Now there are many ways to compensate an employee, there's financial compensation where you pay someone a salary, you can offer them a raise when they do well, you can give them a bonus at the end of the year, but financial compensation is usually not the biggest motivating factor for most people. Remember, most people who have a job are there because they simply want to be able to pay their bills, have some extra money for spending, they want to go on an annual vacation, and that is the extent of their financial interest. They're not looking to become wealthy; otherwise they might want to start their own business. Now everyone dreams about becoming wealthy and everyone would love to win the lottery, but there is a big difference between someone wanting to become wealthy and someone else being primarily interested in financial compensation.

Some of the best ways to reward employees is by giving them some of the products or services that your company provides for free, giving them to them at a highly discounted rate, or giving them other benefits. There are many corporations that offer a free health club membership to their employees, this way employees know that when they come to work at this company, they'll also be able to enjoy a gym which they might otherwise not be able to afford a membership. It might be that they don't go ahead and buy a membership to this gym on their own because even though they have the money, they would rather spend their money on other things. But once they have access to that gym, they'll fall in love with they gym, they'll love the fact that they can work out whenever they want and then they'll realize that the company for which they work is great, because not only does it provide a good salary but it also provides a membership to a great sports gym which they can use to work out and go swimming.

Millionaire business owners know that there are other ways to reward their employees such as a free dinner certificate for an employee and an employee's spouse, a free vacation for the top-performing employee at the company, free usage of a car for the "Employee of the Month", holiday presents. There are many forms of compensation that you can give to an employee. millionaire business owners know that how the compensation is given to the employee is very important also. If you give the compensation to the employee in a way that the employee feels appreciated then the employee feels that he or she really deserves what you are giving them and will appreciate what he or she is receiving a lot more and then he or she will feel obligated to want to work even harder to show you how happy they are that you were able to give them such a great gift or a great bonus. Sometimes a financial compensation such as an extra year-end bonus doesn't do the trick. The reason that it doesn't is because let's say someone receives a bonus of $1000. That $1000 is great, but if the person puts it in his bank account and he soon sees that $1000 disappear since he had to pay his credit card bill, make payments on his furniture that he bought, had to pay for a course he's taking in graduate school, whatever the reason, once that $1000 is gone, the person won't really remember the fact that they received an extra $1000. But instead if you gave someone a vacation that was worth $1000 and let's say the vacation was an all-expenses paid trip to Las Vegas for three days, that employee would have the memory of being in Las Vegas gambling, seeing the sights, and having a great time meeting new people. Those experiences would remain with the employee for a long time; the memories would be clearly in the mind of that employee when that employee came back from his trip. Not only would the organization benefit from having a rejuvenated employee who is now going to work very hard in the business and be very devoted to the business, think about the effect on all the employee's coworkers when the employee goes ahead and tells his or her coworkers what a great vacation he had…imagine how excited those employees will become. Those employees will say "Wow, I would love to have a similar experience in Las Vegas and I will work extra hard this quarter so I can meet the goals that I need to meet in order to receive that free vacation to Las Vegas.

You see when you compensate an employee and you show an employee how much you like him, the employee is not the only one who notices but it's also the coworkers of the employee noticing also. When you make an employee an "Employee of the Month" and give him a special award for a gift, I guess a night out at a fancy restaurant where you give him two tickets to a nice Broadway show, all the coworkers of that employee will say "Hey, you know what, I would like to take my wife to that show, I would love to take my children to that show, I would love to go that fancy restaurant, you know what, I'm going to put in some extra effort this month because I want to be the "Employee of the Month" this month so I can go ahead and enjoy a free dinner at a fancy restaurant and enjoy free tickets to a Broadway show." You see the benefit is also not only for coworkers, but sometimes we give out to the spouse or the relatives of the employee who receives that bonus. The relatives and the family in this case of that employee will be so happy that they'll be able to enjoy that dinner at a fancy restaurant and that they'll be able to go see a fancy show on Broadway that they're going to encourage the employee to work even harder the next month so they can receive tickets again to the Broadway show. They're going to want to work very hard so they can again receive a certificate to go to a fancy restaurant. Think about it, once the wife is happy and the wife likes the results of her husband's employment, she's going to encourage her husband to continue that employment and to work even harder. The same takes place with the husband whose wife is working in an organization. The husband's going to want to encourage his wife to work even harder so that they both can enjoy the benefits of the wife's employment with that organization or that company. The same takes place if you use contractors, if you use independent sales representatives, or if you delegate out work. Let's say that you have a contract with a service provider and that service provider says to you that he or she will continue to make 500 sales calls for you every week in exchange for $300 per week. Now that $300 a week is a good payment, you know it's part-time work contracted by a student or a retiree and they can use that extra $300 a week. But imagine how much more excited that retiree or student would be if you said to them "You know what? Besides the $300 per week that I'm going to pay you, for every week that you're able to make not 500 phone calls, but make 550 phone calls, I'm going to give you a free gift certificate for $25 to Barnes & Nobles." It's not just the money that would encourage, it's not just the value of the gift certificate, but it's the fact that the reason people like to read and that people like shopping at Barnes & Nobles, and people will be excited that they'll be able to receive the $25 gift certificate that they can now go to Barnes & Nobles to do some shopping and get some books that they would enjoy. What if you said to the person doing the cold calling "You know what, for every extra sales lead, for every person that you speak to on the phone who is actually interested in my product or service, every time you have at least twenty people, I am going to give you a $50 gift certificate to go shopping at Macys." Now you know what the conversion ratio of your business is, you might know that for every five people you speak to about your business who have expressed an interest in your business; you have been able to close one sale that gives you a profit of $500. If you're able to get a profit of $500 and it costs you a $50 gift certificate to Macys, then I think you'll definitely agree with me that it's worth it. Remember the more ways you can motivate someone to work harder and the more ways you can move away from financial compensation it will also mean that you'll save money for your business. You'll save money because you won't have to take as much money from your pocket and at the same time the person receiving that benefit will feel a lot better about what it is that they're receiving. For the most part people don't want to receive money as a bonus because they don't want to feel that they're getting a present or a handout. People like to feel that they're working hard and they're getting money only when they truly deserve it. Now most people might disagree with me, most people might say "You know what, people actually like to receive money". You might say that if you were receiving a bonus from your current employer or from anyone with whom you're dealing you would like for it to be money, but I can tell you that while studying millionaire business owners, I was able to see that their preferred form of compensation is not always financial. It is sometime buying their employee a car, buying their top sales person a car, giving their top sales person access to a car, such as in the Mary Kay organization where the top sales person receives free use for one year of the company's pink Cadillac. That's a great benefit because the person is excited about being able to drive a Cadillac throughout the year, having free access to that car, they don't have to buy a car, they don't have to make payments on a car that year, they're driving a brand new car, and at the same time if someone had handed them $5000-$6000 which might be quickly spent in the course of the person's life. Now if someone did hand that person $5000-$6000 there's no guarantee that the person would that money in an activity that would create memories that would help them remember how good it was to be able to work hard to receive the benefit that they receive when they get the compensation.

Remember millionaire business owners always like to compensate people for doing extra hard work or providing an extra great service by giving them something for which memories will last a lot longer than the actual use of the product or service. A free weekend pass to a spa in Arizona is a great benefit because the recipient of that benefit will remember that benefit for a very long time. They'll think about it, they'll look forward to going back again and someone who just received $200, which might be the price for visiting a spa for the weekend, might not actually even use the money for anything. They might just put the money into their bank account and it will just sit there and they'll forget from where that money came or it won't mean as much as actually having enjoyed the spa.

When you start up your business I know that you're not yet at the stage where you can send someone to Arizona for the weekend to enjoy a spa. You might not be at a stage where you are able to buy someone a car. You might not yet be at the stage where you can send someone to a Broadway show, but there are many ways to you to be creative to give people extra bonuses to give your employees an extra incentive to succeed in business. You might give them some extra time off, you might give them a better seat in the office, meaning you might buy the best employees leather seats, meaning the seat still stays in your business, it's still an asset that you own, you still have that seat, but now the employee is happy because they have a better seat on which to sit, a better desk to use, or you can give them a better office within your business with a better view. There are many ways you can compensate employees. You can treat them to lunch, which might only cost you $6 or even $10, but think of how good it will feel for them to be able to have lunch on someone else. Imagine how good they might feel to know that they get to have lunch with their boss. You see there are many ways to compensate employees and the key is to remember that millionaire business owners know that the degree of happiness and fulfillment that their employees have is directly correlated to the level of success a business experiences.

One form of compensation for employees that most employers overlook is letting employees know that and letting contractors know and letting sales people know and letting anyone who does any work for you know or anyone with whom you deal know how much they're appreciated. People want to be appreciated. People want to know that there is a reason for what they're doing and that there is a purpose that they are fulfilling. The nature of a person is to want to know that in whatever activity they are involved that it has a purpose, that it's an important purpose, and that whatever they're doing is essential and important to the running of that organization. People want to know that they're involved important pursuits which are well-viewed by other people. If you want to make sure that your employees are happy and that your employees stay with your business for a long time, you want to make sure that you have hardworking sales people, whether they're the employees of the business or they're independent sales reps, you'll have to find and follow the example of millionaire business owners in always encouraging your employees by always letting your employees know that they're appreciated and by explaining to them what it is that they're doing, why it is that they're doing it, and what the benefits are of what they're doing are to the organization, to the employees of the business, and to the world as a whole.

You see many times someone could have a job as simple as assembling furniture. If you explain to the employee why assembling that furniture is important, why assembling it the correct way is extremely important, who will use this furniture, how will people use this furniture, why people prefer using this certain type of furniture, and why the correct assembly of this furniture is important to the customer, you'll have an employee who will work a lot harder assembling this furniture and will do a much better job assembling the furniture and the employee will understand the importance of his or her job. See, importance is the key word. Importance means that people see the value of what it is that they are doing. The more value that people see in what they're doing the more they'll want to do what it is that they are doing and the more effort they'll put into what they're doing. So keeping your employees happy and content is very important. You can do this by appreciating them, by treating them well, by taking their sides in any customer-employee disputes, and by always treating them fairly, by giving them a high level of training, by giving them jobs that are important, by delegating, by allowing them to feel that they have an important role in the business, and by ensuring that in every stage of the business development that your employees are well-informed of what it is that the business is doing.

See a lot of employees lose morale when there are changes within the business of which they are not aware. When they see change take place, whether or not there's a reasonable explanation for the change, they very often assume the worst and that's when rumors start spreading. The rumor could be as bad as that the company is going out of business or maybe the business is going to be taken over by another company and some of us might lose our jobs, the business doesn't need us anymore, or the business wants to sell new products or services. Whatever the reason is that you are selling that product or service or any reason you are changing that product or service or any changes that you are doing in your business should always be explained to your employees. They should always feel that they're integral members of the team.

Remember how before we mentioned the team? The team is important because a team means that each person is helping the other person of the team succeed, but the way that a person feels if they are part of a team is that they realize that they are part of an organization and that the members of the organization are open with them when they discuss business issues with them, when there is an exchange of communication, and when they're well-informed of any changes. You don't want to leave doubt in an employee's mind or a customer's mind. Anytime there is doubt, doubt ferments negativity, and negativity leads to poor results in customer-employee relationships, in employer-employee relationships, and in service providers to the people to whom they're providing relationships.

In order to have a well-run organization and to have satisfied employees, you need to be well-informed of what kind of changes are coming.

Even if you need to let go some of your employees or even if you need to cut back on the hours that they're going to be working or you need to reduce the commission that you're paying out to independent reps, it's very important to explain to them what it is that you're doing and why you are doing it. If you can provide people with a good solid reason with why it is that you're doing what you need to do, even if your action might impact them negatively to some degree, if they feel that you and I are going out of our way to really explain things to them and they realize that really we have their best interests in mind, they will probably still want to continue having a good relationship with you because they'll perceive you in a very good light.

Millionaire business owners, even when they're forced to lay off employees, go out of their way to give their employees enough warning time so that the employees can start looking for other jobs and they help their employees look for other jobs. They do this for very practical reasons because they know that an employee who knows that he is being fired but knows that his boss or her boss is going to put a lot of effort into helping him find another job, that employee is going to want to do a better job during their remaining time with the company because they're going to want their employer to help them find a good job, are going to want the employer to give them a good recommendation, and are going to want the employer to write them good letters to use their contacts to help them get a job. But if you don't tell your employees that you're going to have to fire them soon, those employees will either at the end when they're actually fired will become very upset and they won't do any work at the end or if they pick up on anything or if they hear a rumor that they're going to be fired then they're not going to work the same way because they're going to feel that they're being mistreated by not being alerted to the fact that they'll soon be losing their jobs.

Millionaire business owners are aware that successful employee-employer relationships consists of an open flow of communications and they're always comprised of employees and employers who feel comfortable approaching each other anytime in discussing any matter that comes up. Millionaire business owners know that employees are sometimes a business of their own, meaning that they can generate business that the owner of the business might not have and might not be able to generate on his own and they might bring the company to new opportunities and to new areas of business of which the company was not previously aware. Millionaire business owners also know that they need to treat contractors, they need to treat independent sales reps, they need to treat anyone in their business to whom they give work as if that person is an employee of their company. That person needs to be compensated fairly, needs to be encouraged fairly, and needs to be included as part of the team of the organization.

7

Millionaire business owners never rest on their laurels. Millionaire business owners know that in order for them to succeed in their business, they need to always constantly grow their business. There is no better way to grow your business than by always bringing in new customers. Millionaire business owners realize that in order for their business to succeed and that in order for their business to grow, they need to always be in a mode in which they're searching for new customers. They always need to be able to bring new business into their business, they always need to be able to increase their revenues, and they always need to sell more not to just existing customers but to new customers. You see any business that wants to succeed has to always bring in new customers so that they can sell to new customers.

Now the reason why millionaire business owners are not satisfied with just selling more to their current customers is because they want to diversify their revenue base. For instance, if a millionaire business owner has one hundred customers and those one hundred customers are giving that business a $400K or $500K a year profit, that's a lot of money for the business to make. But if out of those one hundred customers, if twenty of those customers leave you, let's say five of them go bankrupt, another five of them switch to another competitor, another five of them just exit the business, and another five take a break and don't use the millionaire business owner's products or services, that millionaire business owner now has lost 20% of his revenues and 20% of his profits. In order to avoid that situation, the millionaire business owner would want to always make sure to bring in new customers in case he does lose some customers that percentage wise, he has lost less than if he had less customers

Millionaire business owners also realize that there's not just a chance that they might lose some customers during the next year or so, but they know that the way that life works is that every year they will lose a certain amount of customers. No matter what they do, it is normal for a certain amount of people in business to switch to another competitor, to stop using the product or service that they're currently using, or to simply exit the business. Millionaire business owners prepare themselves for this situation by always increasing their customer base. The more they increase their customer base, also the less they have to depend on any given customer. Many customers take advantage of their suppliers by using their buying power to negotiate and by using their position to leverage themselves into getting a better deal.

Let's say Wal-Mart is ordering from a small wholesaler in Nebraska. Wal-Mart knows that they can drive down the price that they are paying this wholesaler because they say to themselves "Look, we are a very large company, we mean a lot of business to the small wholesaler, we're currently buying 30%-40% of the output that this wholesaler is producing, so we can therefore keep negotiating on the price because if the wholesaler every says no, we take our business elsewhere and the wholesaler loses 30%-40% of his business."

Let's say you own a restaurant in which you receive all of your paper goods from one supplier and then you discover that this supplier is having a very hard time finding customers and you're one of its few customers. As a matter of fact, this supplier of paper goods only has another three customers besides you so you represent 25% of that supplier's business. You now have a lot of leverage to negotiate on the price because if you leave and take your business elsewhere, this supplier is going to have to find someone else to make up for the 25% of the business that he's lost when you left him. You don't want to put yourself into the same situation as that supplier. You never want to be in a situation where any of your customers represent a significant portion of your business. You always want to make sure that your business is spread out among many customers. You could have one customer who orders a lot from you as long as you have many other customers who together also represent a sizeable portion of your business.

Let's say you are the wholesaler in Nebraska and Wal-Mart is buying a million dollars worth of watches every year. Now that's great that you have one customer that's ordering a million dollars worth of watches from you, but what your goal should be is to have another hundred customers who are also ordering a combined million dollars worth of watches a year from you. This means that if you do lose Wal-Mart as a customer of your business which will cut your business in half, you'll still have enough business to support yourself and to make a great profit from the rest of your customers. Successful manufacturers know that in order for them to succeed in their business they always have to have a diverse customer base so that they can supply what they manufacture to many customers and they never have to go under if one of their customers switches to another company or competitor or if one of their customers exits the business.

Millionaire business owners know that the best solution for ensuring that they never over-depend on one customer or on a few customers is to continuously look for more customers that they can continuously look for more customers that they can add to their database so that they can increase their revenues and spread out their sources of revenues from two customers to many different customers. Millionaire business owners realize that the process of looking for new customers is also a great learning experience for them. The more they interact with potential customers the more they will know what it is that customers are looking for, what kinds of products or services they need, what features they want the products to have, what elements they want the services to have, what price they're more comfortable paying, they'll know whether they're charging too much or too little, and they'll be able to understand the business better. By understanding the business better, they'll also be able to provide a higher level of service to their current customers. Let's say you're that wholesaler or you're that manufacturer that produces microwaves for restaurants, the more you interact with potential customers, the more you'll know what kind of microwave for which they're looking. You will know if you're offering the best kind of microwave to the market. See many times your existing customers might not tell you what it is that they need or for what they're looking. Your current customer might feel that right now this is actually all you have to offer and the only reason they might not be going elsewhere is because they feel it is just too complicated to look for another service provider or a product provider, such as in this case. The risk to that is that there is some point at which someone can come along and offer a microwave with the features that they need and if you're not aware that they're looking for this particular feature on their microwave, then you'll never produce it for them.

So millionaire business owners always make sure to not only consult with their current customers, but to consult with potential customers so that they can review the products or services that they're offering and they can determine if they're offering what is best for the custom-ers. If they're not offering what is best for their customers, then they could decide how they will go about offering what their customers truly need. Millionaire business owners know that the lifeblood of any business is its customers and that in order to continue holding onto the customers that it has had in the past and that in order to attract new customers, they always need to stay in touch with those who will be using their products and services so that they can know how to adapt their products or services to the needs of the marketplace. Once they are able to adapt their products or services that they offer to the mar-ketplace, they'll be able to hold on the customers that they have and they'll be able to attract new customers and they'll also always be able to stay a step ahead of their competitors.

You have to realize that what differentiates most business owners from millionaire business owners is that millionaire business owners put in that extra effort to always look for new customers and enjoy the benefits of the increasing business and also the increase in knowledge that meets their needs. That is why there is such a thing as millionaire business owners and business owners who are not nearly as successful as millionaire business owners. So remember to ask yourself what you want to be and how you think that you'll get there. Remember no business should ever be satisfied with the level of business that it has, the only time to truly rest in business is when you're retired and you have the time then to discuss the activities of your business, and to discuss the stories and experiences that you've had, but when you're actively involved in your business, never assume that your customers are okay with you, especially in today's competitive marketplace you can never count on any customer's business for life. The only thing that you can do is to be sure that you do develop a system and develop a system that will help you modify your products and services and encourage that customer to stay for life and see that you find more customers that stay with you the long term to find new additional customers to increase your revenue base. That is the way large companies enjoy the Fortune 500, by continuously learning what their business needs and by continuously looking for new businesses that will bring in more revenue for their company. millionaire business owners are obviously successful in their strategies, and this is one strategy of which millionaire business owners are aware, so always make sure that you're on the lookout for customers.

8

In order for a business to be successful, we've already established that it needs to have customers, and that it needs to always be on the lookout for new customers, but what else does a business need to take into account with regards to customers in order to become successful. Well millionaire business owners realize that the value of a customer is not measured in the sale that is made to a customer or in the profit that the initial sale generates, but that it is the lifetime value of the customer that is important.

See a millionaire business owner bases the strategy of his business on the lifetime value of a customer. The millionaire business owner knows that while each sale that goes through to a customer or each purchase that a customer makes or each transaction that takes place between a business and a customer, whether it's a business-to-business transaction or a business-to-consumer transaction, regardless of the type of transaction, regardless of the dollar-size of the transaction, regardless of the profit-size of the transaction, the real value of a customer is what is called the lifetime value of the customer. You see, when you do business and you sell socks or you sell a car or you sell an airplane to a customer, what you really want is not just the initial sale from that customer, you want to make sure that the customer continues to buy from you, that the customer likes you, that the customer likes what he or she is receiving from you, and feels a certain amount of loyalty or gratitude and will want to continue buying from you. When you have a more long-term view towards business, you'll wind up making a lot more money. The reason is that the lifetime value of a customer means that the value of a customer isn't just the initial sale but is rather every sale that will take place because of this customer and to this customer throughout the life of the customer.

For example, let's say that you have a small restaurant and the average bill per meal is $25. If a new customer comes into your restaurant and he's very demanding or he wants to try a different food or has a lot of questions for you, and at the end, the customer only leaves $25 for the meal; your profit on $25 might only be $6-$8, which is really not a lot of money. So you might become discouraged and say that it's really not worthwhile to be involved in the business because it's a lot of hassle for an $8 profit. What if you're in the retail business and you have a 99-Cent Store where the profit per item is maybe 30 cents, if you look at your customers as lifetime customers, the you'll realize that it is possible to make a good amount of money from your customers. With the example of the restaurant, when you have that argumentative customer or that difficult customer who results in an $8 profit, if that customer walks out of your restaurant satisfied and the customer enjoyed the experience and liked the food and decides to come back and then the customer becomes a regular customer, and let's say on average he comes in your restaurant once a week, so that now is 52 times per year. Fifty-two times a year times $8 a meal because we were saying that you were going to be receiving an $8 profit per meal, the customer's coming in once a week for the 52 weeks per year, so 52 x $8 is $416. So the actual profit value of that customer is $416. If you only looked at the customer for the value of the initial sale, which is $8, that customer really would not be worth much to you from a proper perspective. If you look at that customer and look at his lifetime value and let's say that every year that customer is going to mean $416 profit to you, then you'll take that customer a lot more seriously and you'll be more encouraged to service that customer the right way.

So the key is to always have the right attitude because millionaire business owners know that the real money that they make doesn't come just from the initial sale and from the initial transaction, but it comes from the lifetime transactions that they will be having with the customer. That's why there are many businesses that are willing to take an initial loss on the first transaction only to have a lifetime relationship with that customer. There are many cable companies that will give you the first month free because they know that once you try out their service you'll be happy with their service and you'll continue being a subscriber for good.

Now if a cable company charges you $30 a month to have access to their 500 and plus channels and they give you the first month for free, well first of all their only cost will be the installation costs and let's say they give you the free installation so their not actually offering you a product on which they're losing money because it's just as easy to beam out their cable or to feed their cable through the lines to a thousand homes as it is to send it out to a thousand and one homes. And the installation does cost them money, meaning that the first month they're going to incur a loss, they're going to have to pay the service person $50-$60 to install the cable or the small satellite dish, whichever the case may be for you. If it cost them $50, okay you know now that they're initially taking a loss on you and if they're only getting $30 a month from you for your cable subscription, from that $30, even if there's a high profit, let's say their profit is $25 a month or its $20 a month, they're actually making percentage-wise, a good profit. At $20 a month, they're making approximately 2/3, which is 66.6% profit on the transaction, so at a $20 a month profit then it's going to take them two and a half months to recuperate the expense of installing the cable at your home. Now remember that they gave you the first month's subscription for free, so they'll rather than having to wait then two and a half months, they'll actually have to wait until the end of the fourth month until they have actually started seeing a profit from you. But you see the reason why it's worth it for the cable company is because if you do remain a subscriber for a year there's still another eight months wherein they'll be making another $20 a month profit each month from you. Eight times $20 is now $160 so for the year, you as a customer mean $160 of profit for them. When you look at the transaction now over the course of a 5-year period, the first year their profit is $160, the next four years, the profit each month is $20 a month and 20 x 12 months is $240, and $240 times four is $960, plus the $160 for the first year, which gives us now $1120. So that means that the profit from you over the course of five years is $1120, so I think it would be fair to say that it's worth it to them to give up $50 initially and to give up the profit from the first two or three months which is the time it takes them to recuperate the cost of giving you the free cable installation for having the ability to maker over $1100 from you over the next five years. If the cable company has 1000 customers, over the course of five years, those 1000 customers will have made $1.1 for them in profit.

You see millionaire business owners are willing to give up their profit initially or even to sell at a loss when they know that the lifetime value of that customer will return the money that they have spent upfront for the customer many times over during the duration of the customer's lifetime relationship with the business. Cellular phone companies have followed this practice for a long time. They give out a free phone which costs them money, sometimes even when the cellular phone company doesn't have a deal for a free phone, retail outlets that sell and offer cellular phone service will offer a free phone. The reason the do that is for the following reasons, the cell phone costs them about $50 to buy from their wholesalers, they know that for ever subscriber that they're able to bring to AT&T or to BellAtlantic or to Verizon or any cellular phone service provider, they will receive a commission between $150-$250. That type of a commission is worth a lot to them because look, even if in order to get the commission, they have to spend $50 by giving a customer a free phone, but as soon as they give that customer a free phone, meaning as soon as they have given away that phone that costs them $50, they're going to be receiving from the cellular phone company $150. Now if they do this every month 100 times, which is possible for cellular phone dealers with a lot of volume, they're going to be making over $10,000 a month of profit. Millionaire business owners always follow this example.

Now what savvy millionaire business owners do, and these are the millionaire business owners who really go ahead in their business and take their business to even bigger proportions, they look for services or products they can offer that will hook in the customer, that will make the customer very excited and will make the customer want to stay with them for a long time, but at the same time will not mean a lot in terms of cost to the owner of the business. Millionaire business owners are willing to spend money to appeal to customer and are willing to take a loss initially in a customer to have the lifetime business from a customer, but their cognizant to the fact that you don't always have to sell at a loss in order to have a long-term relationship with your customer, millionaire business owners put into their calculations, into their profit formulas what the cost of that customer is and what profitability they will derive from that customer. For example, it might cost them $50-$60 to advertise to bring in every new customer, meaning that on average if they want to have 20 customers, they'll have to spend at least $1000 in advertising bringing in those 20 customers. But what if they're selling a product that per customer only gives them a profit of $50? Then at best, they have just broken even because it cost them $50 in advertising to bring in that new customer and they only receive $50 in profit from that customer.

So how do they make the business worthwhile? Well they say to themselves "Am I offering a product or service which a customer wants or will want to use in the future and if they're willing to use it in the future, am I offering a product or service that will mean that I will have their loyalty and that will ensure that they will want to do business with me in the future?" Let's say that they're selling vitamins. These are vitamins that you're sure that once your customers use, they'll want to place a reorder and that they will always want to obtain more vitamins. If that's the case, then the millionaire business owner will be willing to advertise, even if the initial order for this customer will only result at best in a break-even scenario, or will result in even a small loss initially, because they know that in the future that customer will want more vitamins from them. Book-of-the-Month clubs do the same thing, they allow customers to receive books free initially because they know that once the customers become members who enjoy receiving their books in the mail on a monthly basis that the customers will get used to ordering books every month and they'll make their money in the long term. Millionaire business owners apply this strategy. They say to them, "It's not enough just to make money the first time from a customer, so I don't need to situate my business in a way that I have to make money from the first transaction."

Many times millionaire business owners will say to themselves that they only want to be in a business where the customer becomes loyal and the customer keeps buying from them. You see if a customer keeps continuing to buy from the owner of the business then the owner of the business doesn't have to look for new customers to continue his business moving. Now millionaire business owners as we've said before will continually look for new customers to grow the business, but the best type of situation to be in is one in which your need from the customer is only based on the need to make more money, not on the need to keep the business solvent. You don't want to be in a situation where you always have to look for new customers or else your business will have to shut its doors tomorrow. Millionaire business therefore, will look for businesses in which once they have a customer, that customer will stay with them for a long time. The wholesale business is similar in this regard. Once you become a supplier of a certain product or a certain service and you offer a high quality item at a reasonable price, your customers will want to stay with you for the long term. Instead of having to always look for new customers, you'll be able to count on a solid base of customers to whom you can deliver merchandise on a weekly or a monthly basis. The same takes place with cable companies that offer cable, the same takes place with cellular phone service companies, long distance companies where they know that once they find a customer and they offer a good product or service at a competitive price and they offer a high quality product or service, they'll be able to count on the continued business from this customer.

Wouldn't you rather be in a situation where once you found a customer you're able to continuously derive income from that customer instead of always having to look for a new customer? Well of course you would and how good would it be if every time you found a customer, that customer would stay with you for the rest of the year and would continue finding new customers who would also stay with you during the rest of the year? You see how much faster your business would grow? Millionaire business owners develop a strategy wherein they keep track of the e-mails of all of their customers. They compile a mailing list of addresses, they will have a contact list with phone numbers, e-mail addresses, they'll have a description of what their customer needs, what their customer wants, what kinds of products and services they deliver or supply to their customers, so that this way they can always keep in touch with their customer and turn that customer into a lifetime customer.

Let's say you have a grocery store and you're selling sodas, oranges, bananas, apples, paper plates, and any other variety of products. In the grocery business, it's very hard to have a lifetime relationship with a customer because if that customer comes in one day he might just be coming because it's convenient while he's running by and he'll come in and pick up a bottle of Sprite. The customer goes home, enjoys his Sprite, and two days later he forgets where he bought the Sprite, and the next time he needs soda, he goes by another supermarket and he stops over there. But if instead he has a grocery store owner who kept the e-mail address and you kept on sending that customer offers on a weekly basis about discounted merchandise, he might then make a special trip to return to your store because he will want to see what other specials you have and the customer will be responding to the offers that you are sending him and he will want to take advantage of those offers. Then that customer doesn't just become a customer who bought a bottle of Sprite, but becomes a customer who stopping by your store on a weekly basis. Let's say he's used to buying $20 worth of groceries which comes out to $80 a month or $960 a year. So over your lifetime relationship with that customer will not mean a bottle of Sprite once in awhile to you, but will now mean to you $960 over the course of a year.

Millionaire business owners that are involved in the car business, whether it's leasing cars or selling cars, whether it's new cars or used cars keep this idea in mind. They never take advantage of a customer. They never look for the quick profit that comes from the sale of one car, but they say to themselves "Maybe this customer is buying an entry-level car from me, he's buying a very basic economy car, I am going to make a decent amount of money from this customer, but I am going to be sure to give the customer the best car that I can because I know that when it's time for this customer to upgrade his car, I know that at the time when the customer earns more money and will have a larger family and will need more room for his family and will want to upgrade to a fancier or a larger automobile, that since I treated this customer well, this customer will remember me and will come back to me. If during the lifetime of the average consumer, the consumer buys four different cars and each car gives the dealer a profit of $3000, then the lifetime value of that customer to the car dealer is $12,000. What a millionaire business owner who is in the car business would do is to develop a good relationship with his customers and he would say to himself "Even if I don't make even $3000 profit from the sale, even if I give them a really good deal and I give them the best car that I can and I only make $2500 on each transaction, but I know that on average each of these customers throughout the course of their lives will buy four cars from me. Four times $2500 is $10,000 profit. If I just have twenty or thirty good customers who over the course of their lifetimes, will buy from me four cars, then the thirty customers times $10,000 will mean $300,000 profit. If over the course of my lifetime as a car dealer, I have two hundred customers and these two hundred customers give me $10,000 profit on average because they're all buying four cars, then those two hundred customers represent a $2 Million profit over my lifetime.

So you see, the key in business is to be able to look at your business as a lifetime business venture. You might not want to do the business you're doing for the rest of your life, but realize that you need to look at it as a long-term business if you want to succeed. millionaire business owners know that the more of a long-term approach that they take towards their business, the more they will be able to succeed because their business strategies are more realistic, and taking into account the nature of people, that people like to shop at the same places, they like to eat at the same places, they like to wear the same type of clothing, they like to deal with people with whom they're familiar, they like to deal with people whom they trust, so if you develop long-term relationships with your customers and you institute a strategy that allows for a long-term relationship with your customer, it will lead towards enabling you to enjoy the benefits of having a lifetime customer relationship. Millionaire business owners are very savvy in this regard.

For instance, if the millionaire business owner is a real estate broker, meaning he's in the process of selling houses, he is aware that 25% of the population of the United States moves every year. Think about what that means. That means that at any given point, there is a tremendous amount of people moving, but what it also means is that if 25% of the people in the country are moving and we can safely also say that it's not the same 25% of the people who are moving every year, it means that every two years, or every five or six, or every ten years, someone with whom the real estate broker is dealing will be moving. I think that I have even read that on average, people move once every eight years. The real estate broker is in the business of selling homes and he right now is selling a home for an owner of a two-family home and he finds a family that wants to buy the home because they want to live downstairs and rent the upstairs to another family. He makes sure to deal fairly with the family, he's honest with them and tells them the benefits of this specific house, the downside of this specific house, what the pros and cons of this location are, the values of the surrounding neighborhood, and he's very fair and honest with them about that house so that they'll feel comfortable with the relationship that they have had with the broker. Then when it comes time for them to sell their house which could be eight years later, they'll want to deal with this broker because they've had a very good experience with this broker. The real estate broker will do the math and he will say to himself that his average commission for a house is 6% of the selling price of the house. If the average price of a house that he sells costs $300,000, then his average commission is $18,000 for the sale of a house. If he figures that the people with whom he deals move on average every eight years, then for every satisfied customer that he has if he could continue working with that person, even if that person will only sell two homes during the person's lifetime, that's a $36,000 commission then, based upon the average example. If he has during the course of his lifetime as a real estate broker fifty customers like that then he will make over $1.5 Million during his lifetime running his business. If that $1.5 Million was being made throughout his career, but it also allowed him to take that money as it was coming in and to invest it into his other pursuits and into other areas that helped him increase his wealth. See millionaire business owners don't mind spreading out their earnings over the course of the years because they're taking that money and they're reinvesting it into their business or investing it into other business ventures that help add to their financial bottom line by helping them make more money.

So if you want to emulate millionaire business owners in this regard, look at what the actual value of your customers are to you over the lifetime of their interactions with you and look at what the potential lifetime interaction is regarding those customers. Say to yourself when you're having a bad experience with a customer "If I make this customer happy and I go out of my way to make sure that the customer walks out satisfied, even if it means refunding the money for the initial sale, how much more money will I make from this customer throughout my lifetime interaction with this customer?" You can make plenty of money by having this attitude. Many people look to make a quick dollar but then they soon find themselves out of customers and out of sales leads from which they can make money. On the other hand, there are people who believe in having more long-term relationships and those people are usually able to find themselves in situations where they always have customers to whom they can sell and suppliers from whom they can buy. People who look at their suppliers from a short-term relationship outlook will negotiate their price very hard and will sometimes play games with them and even though they might get a very good deal initially, they'll then burn bridges and they won't have anyone from whom they can buy and from whom they will obtain the merchandise that they need to sell.

Successful individuals who have a long-term relationship such as millionaire business owners know that the key for them is to have this long-term outlook with regards to the people from who they buy, and in regards to the people to whom they sell. This way they'll be able to be in business for the long term and they'll be able to develop solid, long-term relationships that will deliver lifetime income to them.

9

Every business has to increase revenues and keep a constant cash flow to help the business grow. Businesses also need to keep track of their expenses. Millionaire business owners keep track of every cent and have a system in place to monitor every expense no matter how small that expense. One of the biggest mistakes that people make in business is not being very careful with their expenses and overspend money when it's not necessary. An even bigger mistake which is very easy to make by anyone in business is when it comes to a small purchase or when it comes to a small transaction, it's very easy to ignore the amount of money that is being spent.

Millionaire business owners realize that every expense is cumulative. When they go make a purchase and they see that a $15 item is $2 cheaper at another store, as long as it doesn't cost them too much in time to go to the other store, they would rather go to the other store to buy the item. They will of course do their research before shopping and will only go to the store with the lower priced item, but the reason that they will go to the store with the lower priced item even if they're only saving $2 is not because they need that $2 to live on, but they realize that if they use that attitude towards all of their purchases, the savings will add up.

Look at it this way, if in the course of a business the owner of a business will have to make a thousand transactions and any sort of transactions in which he has to spend money, if on average the owner of that business is able to save $5 on every transaction, that $5 per transaction is not a lot of money. Most of us are probably not that careful when we spend $5, but a millionaire business owner knows that over a thousand transactions, that $5 savings per transaction translates into $5000. Five thousand dollars in his pocket is enough to go on a vacation for a month, it's enough to buy a used car, it's enough to buy a brand new sofa set, it's enough to remodel his kitchen, the bottom is that the money that he saves is the money that he can use by reinvesting in his business or its money that he can use for his person al life. If he is able to take that $5000 and invest it in his business and let's say he buys merchandise that costs him $5000 and which when he sells it, he sells it at a 100% markup so that he can double his money, that $5000 will actually become $10,000. If he does that same type of a transaction again and takes that $10,000 now and buys $10,000 worth of merchandise and sells it at 100% markup, he now makes $20,000 in the transaction. What has actually taken place is that the $5000 which he obtained just by saving money on his purchases has now grown to $20,000. The same could take place whether you saved $1000 over the course of a year or whether you saved $50,000 over the course of a year.

The millionaire business owner knows that every dollar that he saves in his business is a dollar that he can spend in his business, it's a dollar that he can use to grow his business, and it's a dollar from which he can generate more revenues for his business. The millionaire business owner is always looking for ways to save money. He is always looking at different products and services seeing which product or service will offer more for his money and which product or service will help him keep more of his money. See sometimes even if a product or a service costs more, that the value that it delivers might be worthwhile enough to justify spending more money on it. For example, if the business owner needs to buy ink to print invoices on his computer, now there could be one cartridge of ink that costs $20 and one cartridge of ink that costs $25, but if the $25 cartridge of ink will last twice as long as the $20 cartridge of ink, he'll actually save more money on it. You see what many business owners incorrectly do is to concentrate too much on the price instead of concentrating on the benefit or the service or the product that they're actually receiving. Don't count things purely in their economic terms, don't look at things purely in regards to how much you're receiving in quantity or in service, but look at it in relation to what you're spending and also what you're actually spending in relation to what you're receiving. Discount stores work this way many times. Sometimes they'll break down products into very small units and charge a higher price than if a person purchased a lot at once. On the other hand, there are places like COSTCO or Office Depot or Home Depot where they sell things in large quantities or they offer more expensive items, but you're actually receiving a lot more for your money. Even though you're spending more money, in the long term though, you're receiving more for your money. Remember the key is not what you receive, but the key is what you receive in connection with the money you are spending. With that being said, with all things being equal, millionaire business owners will always go out of their way to compare prices and to pay the cheapest price that they can pay. If you ever want to see a tell-tale sign of someone who is not really a successful business owner, see how they spend their money. If you see that they're spending their money very freely and that they're not very careful with the expenses that they're incurring, then chances are that this person is not a true successful business owner because a true successful business owner will train themselves to keep track of their expenses.

See the reason that they train themselves to keep track of their expenses is sometimes not just because of the money that they're saving today, but it's because they want to have that disposition towards their money. They want to be trained that whenever it comes to spending money that they're always careful with it. So for example, the millionaire business owner knows that the same way he trains himself to buy a photocopy machine that costs $500 is the same way that he is going to be trained to buy a truck for his business that costs $20,000.

A millionaire business owner knows that the mind does not differentiate between the negotiating of a $100 item or a $10,000 item. As far as the mind is concerned, they're both negotiating process in which the person has a goal of saving money. If the person sets up a formula and learns how to negotiate, he'll be able to apply those skills to a $100 transaction or to a $10,000 transaction. You see it's a whole lot easier also to negotiate over a $100 item than it is over a $10,000 item. The reason is that people can sometimes become intimidated when they're making a large purchase. They might say "Why I'm not even sure that I can even afford this purchase and I really want it.", and they don't concentrate so much on the price, but instead say "Oh no, this is a $20,000 car, if I try to negotiate for this car, I'm going to look foolish, I am going to look like I can't even afford it." Or, the people who sell that $20,000 car will have a lot of experience selling high-end ticket items and you'll have a very hard time learning how to negotiate for that item. Think about it, the people who sell high-ticket items and high-priced merchandise are people who have a lot of experience in that so they have that job and that's why they're able to sell high-priced merchandise, whether it's a high-priced item like furniture, automobiles, airplanes, a helicopter, a piece of property, whatever it is they have experience selling high-priced items. If you want to be able to compete with them, and by competing I mean you want to be able to negotiate and learn how to save money when making those purchases, if you want to learn how to shop for those types of purchases, how to compare different sources for the item you're considering, and if you want to know how to get the best deal when you're buying that item, what you need to do is go ahead and first train yourself where it is easier, where it is less intimidating. I can assure you that it will be a lot easier for you to negotiate over a $10 item than it is over a $10,000 item initially because chances are that the person selling the $10 item is not an intense sales person and is just looking for that sale to make his quick $2-$3 from the transaction and then move on to the next customer. But the same negotiating techniques still apply. If you negotiate over that $10 item and you bring that item down by even a dollar, what you will learn from that negotiating process you will be able to use when you are negotiating over that $10,000 item. While you might not be convinced by what I'm proposing, I can assure you that if you try it out and if you make it a habit to negotiate and to shop for savings over all your purchases, you'll end up unconsciously applying the same methods and skills and strategies that you learned by shopping around, by researching, by negotiating over a price, by comparing prices for large items as when you did the same thing for small items.

Millionaire business owners know this so they continuously shop around, they continuously try to save on their purchases, and they continuously negotiate over what they're buying because they know that:

A. They're going to be training themselves, they're going to learning how to continuously negotiate, they're going to be learning how to continuously shop for better prices, they're going to learn continuously how to obtain a better price, they're going to understand when they're receiving a good deal and when they're not receiving a good deal, and they'll understand what they are receiving for their money. They'll get themselves into the habit of knowing the importance of saving and they'll develop skills in saving money and then in saving the resources that they have at their disposal to use in their business. On the other hand, we have the second option which is…

B. millionaire business owners know that the reason it is important to save money is because every dollar that they save means more money that is going to stay in their pocket. Let's say you started out your business and you said to yourself "I'm going to initially set aside $3000 to get this business launched. I'm going to start working on my own. I'm going to buy just enough merchandise to start my business and I'm purchasing a computer and a fax machine. I'm going to get a second phone line. This is the money that I have for my business; I have $3000 that I can spend in the business." So okay now you go around and you do your shopping. You look for the best computer available, you compare the rates from different local and long distance phone service providers, you find the best source for merchandise, and you're negotiating even after you find the best price, and now instead of having to spend $3000 to set up your business, you only need to spend $2000. Well now that extra $1000 that you set aside you and your family can enjoy the $1000 and you can spend it wherever you want. Or you could take that extra $1000 and buy additional merchandise so that now you've actually obtained more merchandise for the same amount of money than you would have initially and now your business is that much farther ahead. Instead of only working with let's say for example $1000 worth of merchandise, now your business is working with $2000 worth of merchandise.

Remember what that also means. A millionaire business owner takes the money he saves and reinvests it into his business and uses it to buy more merchandise and that merchandise is sold at a profit and then when he goes next time to buy more merchandise, he gets an even better price on the merchandise that he buys and he negotiates and then he sells the merchandise again and he reinvests the proceeds he receives in even more merchandise and then again he looks for a cheaper price and then he sells the merchandise again, what will end up happening is that he will make that much more money in his business because he'll always be increasing the amount of merchandise he can buy, he'll always be making a slightly larger profit on the merchandise that he sells because he'll have been negotiating the price that he pays for that merchandise and he'll make that much more money in the business.

Millionaire business owners know that the two ways to make money in business are by actually selling and also once you sell by stretching out that profit. The way you stretch out that profit is one of two ways, either charge a higher price or pay less for the merchandise that you are selling. In some competitive markets it's nearly impossible to raise your price and in some markets it's so competitive that if in order to stay ahead, you always find yourself lowering your price or giving more for what you're selling. So if you always continuously lower your cost basis for the merchandise that you're buying or obtain in the negotiating process even more merchandise for what you're spending, then you'll be able to have more to sell and you'll be able to increase your business.

Think about this, if every month you're able to find a different supplier or a supplier who can give you a 5% discount on the merchandise that you're buying, and you then take that 5% discount savings and you reinvest it into your business, then in approximately thirteen months, you'll have doubled the amount of money that you're actually making. This is what will happen, over a twelve-month period, that 5% grows to 60% but since it's cumulative, it's worth a lot more than 60% on a cumulative basis is worth closer to 80%-90%, so instead of your profits being low, they'll have grown in interest by that much.

Let's say for example that you have $1000 and out of that $1000 every month you are able to save $50 through negotiating. Every month you take that $50 and you buy $50 worth of merchandise. Here is what will happen, you'll have an extra $50 a month profit which comes to $600, but now every $50 allows you to buy another $50 worth of merchandise also, so you're actually every month now giving yourself the second month you're giving yourself another $100 worth of profit, the third month you're giving yourself another $150 worth of profit, and so on, it keeps building up until you've not only made that extra $600 from having negotiated a better prices on your merchandise, but you have another $600 in your pocket from the increase in profit from every month, so you have $1200 a year now to put in your pocket which is equivalent to more than one month of profitability.

See what you have actually done is you have given yourself an extra amount of profitability without having to work that month, so I'm sure you can see the benefits of seriously negotiating and seriously looking for more ways to save money and to increase the business that you have and the best way to do that is by training yourself in every type of situation to save money and by always monitoring all your expenses. Millionaire business owners monitor and keep track of every expense that they have no matter how small.

Millionaire business owners do not tolerate any employees or any contractors or any consultants who are not careful when it comes to expenses. When you look at many of the promising dot-com companies and the reason I say that is they are promising is because many of those dot-com companies really had something going for them. They really had good business minds and could have made a lot of money if they had good products and if they had been able to take advantage of the lifetime value of their customers they would have made plenty of money. Even though it would have taken them time to reach profitability, if they had maintained control of their expenses, they could have waited and would have seen profitability because even if it had cost them $100 to bring in a customer from whom they barely made a $20 profit, by the sixth transaction with that customer, they would have been at a profit and then every transaction from then on with that customer would have resulted in a profit. So you can see from there that the businesses that were doing business on the Internet, a lot of them that went out of business could have actually persevered and they could have become very successful enterprises if they had monitored their expenses or if they had held enough cash to last them through their operations. See the millionaire business owner says to himself "Even if it's taking me time at the beginning to make money and even if right now the business I'm doing with my customers is not really worthwhile but at some point the profit that those customers give me will add up and during the long term, I'll make a lot of money from the transactions with those customers."

But what happens is that many business people have such high expenses that they're not able to wait while they're incurring expenses and while they're customers are not yet giving them a profitability. You see many Internet companies had such high expenses and were throwing around so much money and were not careful with the money that they were spending, that even when they were sometimes months away or weeks away from profitability, they weren't able to be there, they weren't able to stick around that long because their expenses were so high that they just lost the money that they had to cover their business expenses. Their cash converter rate was so high that some of them were spending upwards of hundreds and hundreds of thousands of dollars a month on their business and they didn't have anything to show for it. You see the problem wasn't that they didn't have anything to show for it now because they were developing good customer relationships that were going to give them millions of dollars of profit in the future, but the problem was that they weren't careful with their current expenses because they thought that they were going to be making the money that they wanted to make much sooner and they figured that even if they went through all the money that they had that they would all soon be making so much money that it just wouldn't be important. If they had slowed down the amount of money they were spending every month and if they had been more careful with the money that they were spending and had spent it only on items that were intrinsic for the business and had monitored their expenses more closely, they would have been able to support themselves with the money that they had invested in them until they reached profitability.

Millionaire business owners know that when they first start out a business that there is no sure way to know when they will be profitable. There is no way to know if it will take them a month to reach profitability, whether it will them six months, or even if it will take them three years, but they do believe in their business. They have very strong convictions and they are sure that they will make money in their business, so what they do is to position themselves in a way so that they're spending very little money initially on their business, they monitor expenses very carefully, they only spend money when they have to, and when they do spend money, they make sure they get the best price possible so they are sure that while their business grows and while they progress to the next stage and they get closer to profitability, they will not have to worry about the risk of running out of money before the reach profitability and before they start bringing in revenues that can cover their expenses.

Millionaire business owners keep track of every expense, even if it's only a $2 expense. If you want to become a millionaire business owner start training yourself to keep track of every expense that you have and start training yourself to negotiate over every expense that you incur. Start training yourself to know how to research, how to develop resources where you can continuously get merchandise, get services, get products at a cheap price, and that you can get those same products and services at the highest level compared to the money that you are spending. Remember it's not enough to get a very good price, but we also want to get the most that we can for our money. Very simply put the more money we save when we buy merchandise, the more merchandise we can buy. The more money we save on our phone bill, the more we can speak on the phone. Every expense takes away from our profitability. Every dollar that we save allows our business to grow that much farther and allows us to have a higher level of profitability. Remember if this strategy is good for millionaire business owners, then it's definitely good for the rest of us. So I wish you luck and ask that you review this chapter making sure that you institute this in the bylines of your company's business plan.

10

One of the most effective strategies that millionaire business owners use is the backend sale. The backend sale is a sale opportunity that is set up after the initial sale. What that means is that not after you sell to a customer you try to contact the customer and sell again, I mean that's an ideal strategy, but that's something that's commonly used and that's a strategy that is a basic strategy and is based upon whether the customer enjoyed his experience or not or again needs a product. Everyone is interested in selling again to a customer in order to make money. Now what is very unique about a backend sale is that the backend sale actually captures the customer's attention as soon as the sale has been made and at that opportunity, another sale opportunity is introduced to make money from the customer. The reason a backend sale is so effective is because since the customer has just had a good experience with you and the customer has just showed you that he is willing to spend money with you, that customer will be more inclined to spending money again. See the reason this is true is because the customer has already overcome his doubts and his hesitancy regarding doing business with you. However it may be, the customer has already been convinced that it is to his or her benefit to make a purchase from you, to buy a product from you or to purchase a service that you provide. Because the customer has already made that positive decision to go ahead and go through the transaction with you, that backend sale is a lot more likely to happen.

See the reason that the backend sale is more likely to happen is that you already have an instant connection with that customer. The customer is already in the mindset of where he or she is already spending money to purchase product or a service. At that point, since they're already spending money purchasing your product or service, they will be more willing to do what they need to do in order to acquire the next product or service. You see your credibility is already established in their mind. The reason that your credibility is already established in their mind is because they have already purchased a product or service from you. And if they have already purchased a product or service from you and they believe in the benefits that the product or service offers, they'll be more likely to again to purchase another product or service from you.

You see, if you sell them a special pot that helps them cook meat in a very quick and timely manner and they buy that pot and then your backend sale is a special seasoning that goes on the meat that they will be cooking in that pot and you tell them that the seasoning is going to give anything that is cooked in that pot, including meat, chicken, fish, or pot roast, a very good, solid taste, what will happen is that they will want to purchase those spices. The reason is that they already believe you and the reason you know that they already believe you in the first place is that they bought the pot from you. Secondly, they're in the mood of buying and so since you already know that they're in the mood of buying and you know that right away they want to experience the being able to cook, they're going to want something that is going to enhance the experience of cooking. In this situation, what is going to enhance the benefits of cooking is the spice that you will be selling along side or in addition to this pot that you are selling them.

There have been studies which have indicated that backend sales work 50% of the time, meaning that 50% of the time that you're able to offer your customer a product or service for sale instantly after they've made a purchase from you that 50% of the time the customer will buy a second product or service from you. Millionaire business owners always make sure that the backend sale product or service is very similar or it is complimentary to what the customer has bought. Let's start out by finding out what I mean by saying "similar". If a customer has just bought a pair of jeans from you and as a backend sale you try to sell that customer sneakers, well there's no assurances that the customer will want to buy the sneakers because first of all the reason he bought the jeans might not have anything to do with the reason why he might buy sneakers. The benefit that he's looking for in jeans is not the same benefit that he's looking to get from sneakers. The type of customer who wears jeans might not necessarily be the type of customer who wears sneakers. The sneakers that you're selling the customer might not be associated with any activities in which he will be wearing the jeans. He might be using the jeans for a casual day at work and he would never consider wearing sneakers at a casual day at work, he might associate sneakers only with playing basketball and he might not be a basketball player. But a similar product to the jeans would be a second pair of jeans at a discount, this way the customer will say "You know what, I was only originally planning on buying one pair of jeans, but now that I see a second pair of jeans being offered at a really great price, I'll go ahead and purchase a second pair of jeans." Another similar type of product would be a shirt offered to the customer that matches the jeans and is commonly worn together with jeans. This way the customer will say "Look, I know that I need a shirt and I know that at some point I need to buy a shirt that matches the jeans, and you know what, I might already have shirts, but this shirt is a really nice looking shirt, it's similar to the type of shirt that I was planning on buying for the jeans, it's a beautiful looking shirt and the people who are selling me the jeans now I know are selling good quality clothing and I am willing to take a chance on their clothing, I enjoy buying their clothing, I plan on buying their clothing because I just purchased the jeans from them, so let me go ahead and with this same assurance and credibility that I feel towards the people who are selling me the jeans, so let me go ahead and buy the shirt from them also." Now a complimentary product could be a special type of detergent that you advertise as being especially good to clean jeans, a stain removal product that works on jeans, anything that would be complimentary to the jeans. If the jeans are Levis®, something you could sell as a backend sale is a men's wallet manufactured by Levis®. The reason that would work is because the customer who just bought jeans, if it's men's jeans, then it's the same customer who needs wallets. Men like to use wallets and if you're selling a pair of jeans for a man or you're selling them to a woman who is buying them for a man, he or she might also way to have the wallet and if the wallet is also manufactured by Levis® and the person just purchased Levis® jeans then he likes the Levis® brand, he enjoys having things made by Levis®, he feels comfortable buying from you and he might buy the complementary product. The key to the backend sale is to make sure that the product that you're selling is either a second unit which is basically the same unit that you sold them in the first place and now the second unit is sold at a discounted price.

The reason you're offering a discounted price is to give the person an extra incentive to purchase a second unit or a third unit or a third unit when they were originally only planning to purchase one unit. You can offer a similar product, a product in which the type of customer who would buy a certain product or service from you would be interested in buying also.

For example if you're selling children's books as a backend sale you might try to sell the parents coloring books because the same parent who would buy the children's books to read their kids bedtime stories at night will also be inclined towards buying coloring books for their children. It's a similar product, it fits the same category, and it provides the same benefit which is entertainment and educational value for their children. Parents are happy to buy it because it's something which they know their children will enjoy and that will make their children happy. Parents will feel comfortable buying their children the coloring books from you because they've just bought the children's books from you. So the key in this type of situation is to offer a product that is similar to the product that you've sold before. Now a complimentary type of product would be once you've sold the parents children's coloring books as a backend sale, offer them a really good deal on colored markers, pens, pencils, or anything that children would use to color in the books. The reason that would work very well is because once again the parents feel comfortable buying from you, they're already buying from you, they're buying children's books and children's coloring books and in order to use those children's coloring books, their kids will need crayons, magic markers, colored markers, and pens. The parents will be happy to buy those products because they're complimentary in nature.

The same example holds true if you're selling college students notebooks, you might want to also sell them calculators as a backend sale. You might want to sell them pens as a backend sale. The key is if you want to be able to have that statistic work for you, the statistic that says that 50% of backend sales are successful, meaning that for every two times a backend sale is offered to a customer, it will result in one sale, you need to make sure that the product you're offering in the backend sale makes sense, that it something geared toward the customer, that it is something the customer will want to have and will want to use.

Millionaire business owners base their entire business on the fact that 80% of the revenue that they'll be producing for their business comes from backend sales and follow up sales. Follow up sales are sales that are done later on that occur in the lifetime of the customer relationship, but the backend sale is a substantial part of that 80%. They know that there's nothing like seeing a customer come into their retail establishment, there's nothing like seeing a company hiring them for an advertising campaign, and at that point they offer them a backend sale or a backend service, and at that time since the customer's in a buying mood the customer will take advantage of the opportunity and will place an order for additional services or an additional product. Let's say you're in a service type of a business. Let's examine what millionaire business owners do in service businesses. If they have a business in which the service is to offer business startup advice and the main product that they sell is the research for and the writing of business plans for anyone looking to get into business. A great backend sale would be one month of consulting services at a discounted rate.

Why would that work perfectly? Look at all the factors that are fulfilled. An entrepreneur who purchases a business plan from this consulting company is looking to start a business. If he trusts this company to be able to provide him good advice in terms of being able to draw up a good business plan, he'll also trust them in regards to listening to its business advice and if he went to them in the first place because he wanted a business plan from them, meaning that he believes so much in their business plan, it will also mean that he'll want to receive from them business advice.

And if in the first place, he decided to purchase that business plan, it means that he highly values that business advice that they can give him and that he wants the business advice that they give him. Now there was a reason why he didn't purchase the business consulting advice from them in the first place. It could be because he couldn't afford the full rate, he wasn't sure yet how much service or advice he would need from them, but once he had already purchased that business plan and he's excited to see that business plan, this would be the time to offer the backend sale and to encourage him to also take them up on that month of business consulting. The business consulting is complimentary, it helps out the business plan, and the offer can be structured so as to say we will help the customer implement this business plan in the first month of operations. That's a great offer because it's complimentary and it's also similar because the customer who purchased the business plan is actually purchasing business advice. And that one month of business consulting advice is also business advice, and the fact that they're offering the first month at a discounted rate will make the customer be convinced to purchase that business consulting for the first month because he'll see what a great value and what a great deal he is receiving.

Another example can even be an attorney. If an attorney is selling a corporate kit and as part of the corporate kit the attorney goes ahead and actually incorporates the business for the people who have purchased the kit and he charges $350 for that service. For that service, people will receive the corporate kit, they receive a corporate seal, and their business is incorporated with the state in which they live. At that point when they feel comfortable using that attorney and that attorney's advice and if they hadn't used that attorney's advice, a great backend sale would be for the attorney to offer to set up their bylaws for them, to offer to give them a lease contract or a sales contract or to draw up any type of a contract that this business would need at a 25% discount. The reason that would be a great backend sale is because a business that incorporates will need contracts at some point, that business might need a lease contract, they might need a lease reviewed when they are about to enter into a lease. If the business is planning on leasing equipment they'll want to have an attorney review the leasing arrangement. If they want to hire someone, they might need an employment contract and if that attorney offers to either give them a contract or review any contract for them as long as they prepay now at a 25% discount, chances are he'll be able to sell that additional backend product, which in this case is a service to at least 50% of his customers. Just think about it, all of his customers know that at some point they are going to need either to have a contract or to have a contract reviewed. They might have another legal matter about which they're not so sure and they might not even end up using this attorney even though they need this service, but they might actually go elsewhere because as time goes on they'll meet other attorneys and meet other people, so it makes sense for the attorney to offer them a 25% discount. If that attorney was the only attorney in town, he would never need to offer a backend sale like this because people would have to come to him eventually when they needed legal services, but since there are so many lawyers around that the customer can easily after using that lawyer for his services could easily go somewhere else and have his contract done by another attorney. Now since he has an offer to receive that legal work at a 25% discount, he knows that at some point he will need legal services, he would probably take that attorney up on the offer. He would probably say to himself "Look, I definitely do need a contract, I will need my contract reviewed, so let me lock in now a great rate at a 25% discount."

Millionaire business owners actively research opportunities to set up backend sales and if they don't have a product or service to offer as a backend sale, they look for products or services in which they can provide the backend sale. Now many times attorneys or CPA's will at a fee recommend other products or services as a backend sale even when it's not their own product or service. They can make deals as long as they fully disclose everything to their clients, they can make deals with third parties to offer a product as a backend sale and receive a commission if the customer goes ahead and purchases a product or service.

Financial planners do this. When they formulate a financial plan for their customers and they charge a fee for the plan, let's say they charge $300 to formulate a financial plan for the client, right after they formulate that financial plan they come back to the client with suggestions and they offer products or services that are based on the financial plan that they've given to the customer. Since the customers do want that financial plan and they've value that financial plan, they will be very likely to want to use the services the financial planner is using and they might pick up the opportunity to purchase the products that the financial planner is offering. Financial planners then are compensated by their own company, but they also receive a commission from the other companies that actually provide the annuities or the mutual funds which the financial planner is selling to make his money.

In any profession, you'll see that people who make money are big believers in backend sales and the people who do use backend sales make even more money and reach the status of millionaire business owners a lot sooner and a lot more often than people who don't work with backend sales. If you want to take advantage of this great millionaire business strategy for your business, you need to first make a list of the true benefits your business provides. Knowing what products or services you provide isn't enough because then you offer a backend sale most of the time you're not offering the exact same product or service again. One strategy which is easy is to just offer the second product or service again at a discounted rate or offer more of the product for the price and hope that more people will purchase as a backend sale so that they can get more of your product or service at a cheaper price.

The problem is that with certain products or services, people don't need the same product or service again even if you offer it at a cheaper price. For example let's say someone is considering purchasing from you a free consultation to draw up a will and then as a backend sale you can't offer to draw up a will for them a second time because they only need to draw up a will one time. The backend sale in that case can be one annual modification to a will at a discounted rate. But you can't just offer another drawing up of a will because people only need a will to be drawn up once. They might need modifications, but they don't need an entirely different will.

If you're selling someone three suits and as a backend sale you want to offer them a fourth suit at a discounted rate, the customer might not need a fourth suit at a discounted rate, and you might not want to offer a fourth suit at a discounted rate because you know that if you don't sell the suit to this customer that you can always find another buyer for that suit. So why offer it at a discounted price? What you want to investigate in this situation is what are the true benefits that the people who are your customers are looking to obtain. The person who is drawing up a will obviously wants to have a very structured life. He wants the security of knowing that his heirs will receive his estate in a very structured manner. That person might need other products or services that you can offer him that would be complimentary. You could set up a trust fund for that person because that would be complimentary since a trust fund also enables assets to be passed on to the second generation.

Now an example with the person who bought the suits from you as a backend sale you could offer matching ties, you could offer matching shirts for the suits, you could offer matching belts for the suit, but the backend sale would have to offer the same benefit for which the person who is buying the initial product or service is looking. So with your business, whether it's a product-oriented business or a service-oriented business, or both, let's say you sell suits and you also offer tailoring on the premises, or you sell computers and you offer set up advice and you offer, for a fee of course to set up computers and to teach the users how to use the computers and how to get the most out of their computers, in that type of a situation, what you would want to do is to offer as a backend sale a product or a service that's complimentary to what the users are looking for from your product or service.

A great backend sale for a computer business would be software that the customers will need when they use their computers. It could be a more advanced class that will teach them how to apply the computer and the software that they have installed on the computer towards their personal lives, towards their business, or towards any personal situation that they have a need for it. With your business, make a list of all the benefits that your business offers to its clients, what your clients are looking for when they interact with your business, what your client's need is in general, the type of clients that come to you have their own specific needs, what are those needs, and then you're going to have to find products or services or you're going to have to develop products or services that meet those criteria.

Once you decide what products or services you want to offer as a back-end sale, if you yourself cannot provide that service, you might want to contract out with a third party and any business that you send to that third party will pay you a commission or you can negotiate a low price with that third party for the service that the third party will be providing to your customers. Then you can go ahead and offer and markup that product or service to make money.

For instance, if you contract out with a web designing school and the web designing school is going to offer your customers as a backend sale or in other words, you're going to be offering as a backend sale web design classes at this institute at a discount. Let's say you're offering those classes at a 25% discount then what you might want to do is actually obtain a 50% discount from the web designing school and that 25% difference is your profit. So if the classes are normally priced at $200 for five sessions and you the provider of those classes, which is the web design school in this case, allows you to purchase the classes from them as you need the classes at $100, then you would mark those prices up to $150. You're still offering your customers a discount, you're offering your customer a 25% discount from what they would normally pay if they went to that web design school and you're making money by making $50 on every transaction. You're making money every time you're able to get a customer to purchase web design classes after they're purchased your primary product or service.

Now you could do the same thing with a product. If you yourself own a men's suits store and you don't want to invest in men's leather coats, but you know that the people who buy suits from you would be willing to buy men's leather coats, you can carry a few of those leather sports coats in your store on a consignment basis. This means that you can have an arrangement with the owner of a store that sells leather coats and tell the owner of the store "Look, let me hold two leather coats at all times in my store, let me hold one at all times in my store. When a customer buys a suit from me, I will right away offer him this leather coat at a discount. If the customer buys it, I will quickly come to you, give you the money for the leather coat whatever money we agreed upon, I will keep of course the difference in the profit and then I will take the next one from you." This way you're offering a very big benefit to the owner of that leather coat because the store that sells that leather coat and the store from which you're getting those leather coats will be very happy because they're going to be able to sell more leather coats than they would otherwise. Even if they're just selling one more a week, that's one more than they were selling before. The benefit to your customer is that he or she is able to buy that leather coat at a discount and the benefit to you is that now you're selling a product that has no cost to you. It's all profit because you're only paying for it after you sell it. That's a great backend sale because it's complimentary to what you're selling and it has the same benefit for which the customer is looking. They want to be dressed very nicely, they want to dress fancy and this leather coat allows them to dress in a fancy manner and it helps them also when they wear their leather suits to protect the leather suits from rain or from adverse weather. You can also contact different wholesalers and ask them what they feel would be a great backend sale that would compliment what you're selling now. These wholesalers want your business and they will be honest with you and tell you what products would fit well.

There are plenty of books where you can find wholesalers who can offer you complimentary products for what you are selling. You can also have what I call a backend sale that's not a product per se or a service pre se but is an offer for a product or service, meaning that you don't have to sell a product or a service as a backend sale, you could send your clientele a gift card offering a discount for a future purchase of a product or a service meaning if you have a clothing store and you're not sure what item your customer needs or the customer themselves is not sure what item they need and you don't want to offer the wrong product as a backend sale.

What you can do after you ring up your customer's purchase, and this is true whether you have a store, whether you have a web site, whether you have a mail-order catalog, whether you have a phone-based operation, whether you have a delivery service where you actually deliver the clothing to your customer's office or at your customer's doorstep, what you can do after the sale is made is offer the customer a gift card and say "This gift card entitles you to purchase $100 worth of merchandise at my store, but because you just purchased from me, I am willing to sell you this $100 gift card at $80, meaning that you're instantly receiving a 20% discount on all purchases because $100 worth of purchases will only cost you $80 when you use this gift card." Whatever type of a situation you're in and whatever type of product or service you're selling, you can always offer people a gift card at a discount.

If people are comfortable using your products or services and they enjoy your products or services, and if they've already made an initial purchase of your product or service, chances are that they would be willing to make another purchase from you in the future. And if they're willing to make another purchase from you in the future, why not give them a way to lock in a lower price now for what you're offering.

Think about it this way. You're a customer who walked into a car dealership. After weeks of shopping around, after haggling over the price, you finally decide to buy a brand new Ford Windstar mini-van. You think that this is an ideal van that accommodates your whole family, there's plenty of space for storage, it rides great, it's extremely comfortable, it's high quality, it has great gas mileage, so you like it and you buy it. After you buy it, the dealer says that he has great accessories that go along with this Ford Windstar. Not only that, but in another three months, you're going to have to change the oil for your Ford Windstar in order to keep it in top shape. Not only that, but on down the line, you might want to go through the normal servicing process where we realign the wheels, we make sure that everything is working. You might want to get your car washed, you might want to have a fancy cleanup job done on your car, what I'm willing to do is since we as a dealership offer all these things, I'm willing now to give you a certificate that allows you to purchase $100 worth of products or services from us at a 20% discount. I'll sell you this card now which is a gift certificate that will allow you whenever you want to come in to purchase anything you want from us up to $100 at a 20% discount. The customer at that point will say to himself "Hey look, I need this car, I obviously just purchased this car because I enjoy this car and I want to be able to enjoy it and to take care of it, and at some point I'll need a car wash and at some point I'll need an oil change, and I might even want to buy some accessories for the mini-van, so let me go ahead and buy this certificate for $20 which will give me a 20% discount on a $100 purchase." It only costs the customer $20, it gives the customer a 20% discount, or you can actually give the customer a bigger discount so that the customer would have the incentive to buy it, so let's say this discount is actually for 30%, so for $20 the customer can receive a 30% discount on future purchases and you might even allow the customer to purchase more than $100 from that certificate. You might even want to make it an unlimited certificate, this way the customer knows that over the course of the next three years he might spend over $500 in oil changes, car washes, accessories, checkups, and tune-ups, and he would like to have a 30% discount on all the products and services that he purchase from this dealership and for $20, it's worth it. Now why would the dealership be willing for $20 to give such a great discount on all products and services in the future? Because the dealership has a profit that's much higher than 20%, the profit margin could be as high as 50%-60% and what it also does is to guarantee the dealership a customer.

Since the customer has already invested money in a relationship with this dealer, then the customer will want to come back and use the certificate with this dealer so that he can get his discount. Think about it, they've already spent money, so they're not going to let the discount go to waste. So instead of going to another dealership to obtain the products or services such as car washes, oil changes, tune-ups, or accessories that they could get from another dealership, they will come back to this dealership and obtain the products or services that they need because they have already invested money and now they want to take advantage of the benefits that this certificate offers such as getting a discount on all their future purchases. In any type of business that you're involved in, I strongly recommend that you set up a system where you can offer a backend sale in terms of a discount card or a gift certificate because since the customers have already purchased from you and the customer is already enjoying the product or service that you offer, they're going to be very likely to want to come back and if you give them a reason to come back, you give them a very strong incentive for savings to come back, then they're definitely going to want to come back.

If you really want to make sure that you lock them and that they do come back, then this benefit, at a cost to them, this way they already feel that they've invested money and they're not going to want that money to go to waste so they will come back to take advantage of this discount or this gift card that you've given them. Anytime that they use this discount card, since they're receiving a discount on their purchases, they will end up spending money on what they are buying from you and you'll have more of a profit in the future. Even if what you are doing is just selling them a gift card at a discount, it's still beneficial.

Let's say you sell a customer a $50 gift card for $40, so you've given the customer a 20% discount and the customer can now go ahead and purchase $50 worth of clothing that will only really cost him $40. So chances are that once the customer comes to your establishment and uses that gift card for $50, chances are the customer will see other things in which he or she is interested. When they see those things they're going to want to buy more from you and at that point, besides the $50 gift card, they might end up spending another $30-$40 buying other items that they see in your store, or ordering other items from your menu, or paying for other services that you offer because they're in the process of buying and they're in the buying mood. They're excited about what their purchasing and they have a need for the products or services that you're offering.

So backend sales work extremely well because they enable you to sell more, they enable you to make more money at the time of purchase, and they enable you to set up a relationship with the customer so that the customer will come back in the future or will feel that they will have to come back in the future to purchase your products or services. Of course, you are not tricking the customer because you're offering the customer something that he truly needs. He or she wants the products or services that you offer, but chances are that as life goes on, they might forget where they bought the product or service and even if they do remember, it might be more convenient for them to shop elsewhere. It might be more convenient for them to get their hair cut at another barber shop. It might be more convenient for your customer to get her nails polished or to have a manicure at another nail salon, but if you at least give them an incentive or you get them to buy a discount card for your products or services, then they will feel inclined to go out of their way even if it is not so convenient for them to come to your nail salon or to your barber shop to get their manicures or their hair cuts because they have already invested something into the relationship.

This is true for any type of a business transaction or business relationship. When both parties have something invested in the relationship, there will be more at stake, and therefore, both parties will be more inclined to continue the relationship and to continue pursuing business together and to continue the "buy and sell" relationship that you need in order for your business to prosper and to continue making money.

If you sell over the phone, the best way to have a backend sale is to taking the credit card or check over the phone, process the order, and immediately offer an additional product or service that is complimentary to what you have just sold. If you are doing it through a catalog, the way to do it is to either fax the customer, or right away to mail the customer another offering that's complimentary to what the customer has just bought from you.

Another great way to do a backend sale is to actually enclose an offer in the product that you're mailing out to the customer, meaning that if you're mailing the customer a box of shoes, you could enclose with that box of shoes an offer for dress socks or for shoe polish. Any product or even a service that's complimentary to what the customer has purchased from you will work. If you have a web site, you can have a page pop up right after the order has been processed for the customer, meaning where the customer puts in his credit card information, the order goes through, and when the "thank you" page pops up with the record number for the customer, so that he can keep track of his order and has a receipt for his order, have an offer on that page of another complimentary product or service that the customer can buy from you. Those are three ways to ensure that you have a profitable backend offer which the customer can act upon while the order is still fresh in his mind.

The mail order is a little more difficult. The one way to get around it is to ask the customer for a fax number and you can instantly fax the customer a backend offer. The way the offer is structured is that you would begin it by saying "Thank you for your order. We really appreciate it and are processing it for you now so that it can soon be shipped to you. While we have your attention, we would like to let you know about some other great products or services that we offer, such as..." and then you'll list the products or services that you offer. If you follow this strategy, you'll be able to turn even a mail order customer into instant repeat customers in terms of customers who will act upon your backend offer.

There are many ways to use a backend offer. If you're doing face-to-face selling, once you've completed a transaction, once you've received payment and handed over or given the service which the customer wants in exchange for the payment, at that point you can offer another product or another service that's similar or complimentary to the product or service that the customer has just obtained from you. Remember the key is that millionaire business owners always make sure that the backend offers are for products or services, sometimes for both, sometimes that are products and services that are similar in nature to what the customer has ordered that are complimentary in nature to what the customer has ordered and are priced lower than they would normally be priced to encourage the customer to act now to purchase it instead of planning to purchase it later in the future.

The question that you address now is whether a backend offer should be for multiple products or services or for only one product or service at a time. After doing some research and consulting with others who are involved in business, I have come to the conclusion that it is much better when conducting a backend offer to only offer one product or one service instead of offering a few different products or services.

The reason is that if you offer more than one product or service, you can confuse the customer and the customer will simply lose interest or even if they are interested, they'll be so confused that they won't be sure which offer upon which they should act. If you limit the choices to one choice, then it's either a yes or a no regarding whether they want that product or service, either they do or they do not. The confusion factor is taken out of the picture. What ends up happening is that the customer doesn't perceive the offer as simply an attempted sale when you offer him more, but the customer sees it as a genuine offer, plus also giving him an additional benefit of the product or service that you're offering. Then the whole business relationship starts when the customer starts to view you not just as a product or a service provider, but as an entity or as a business that really has products or services that are well thought and will match what he or she needs. You see the customer has not been fooled into thinking that you don't want to sell him or her something and that you don't want to make money, but the customer appreciates the fact that you have thought out your offer and that your offer is actually tailored to what he or she needs. If he sees only that you have only one product or service in your backend offer, then he'll think that your company, your business has taken the time to make sure to offer something to him that he actually does need and is something that is similar or complimentary to what he has just purchased. They will see what a serious product or service provider that has what's good for them in mind while at the same time they do realize that you're looking to make money in business, but there's no reason why your desire to sell and your desire to make money can't fit in and be complimentary to your desire to serve the customer well by supplying the customer with good products or good services. But that's business in this country and businesses that are owned by millionaire business owners are all based on this principal of servicing the customer with the best quality products or services priced at the best economically priced level while at the same time with the interest of the business owner in mind, meaning that the business owner wants to be able to make money from what it is that the business owner is offering and there is nothing wrong with that.

The business owner knows that he or she needs to make money and the customer also knows that the business has to make money, but the customer is happy to do business with the millionaire business owner because they know that they're going to be receiving a product or service of very high quality and priced at a reasonable rate compared to what it is that they're receiving. This doesn't mean that you always have to be offering products or services that are priced very cheaply, you can actually charge a very high price as long as it is very clear to the customer that they're receiving an over-abundance of benefits from the products or services purchased for the price that they are paying. If you can do this, if you can clearly demonstrate that even though your product or service is priced higher than the competition or that regardless of what the competition charges your products or services is sure to be expensive, but you're offering a product or a service that will deliver an enormous value to the customer, the customer will not mind spending a lot of money with you because the customer will feel comfortable knowing that they are receiving plenty of value for the money that they are spending.

Another important topic that must be discussed regarding a backend sale is the price at which you're offering. This is truly important because even though the customer is in the buying mood, the customer is interested in what you're offering, and the customer feels comfortable doing business with you, you have to be very careful that you don't break his train of thought, that you don't do anything to destroy the customer relationship because even if the customer doesn't buy the backend sale, you still want him to make a purchase from you in the future.

If you're not careful and you don't go through the process correctly in the backend sale, the customer will decide not only not to buy the backend sale, he might decide to return what it is that he is buying from you, he might cancel the transaction, and the customer might never return and make another purchase from you. So it's very important when you have a backend sale that it's structured correctly. If a customer feels that it's not just a matter of your looking to sell another product but as we mentioned before the customer needs to feel that you are giving him something of value, you are giving him a special benefit because he or she is a customer of yours. The way you do that as by offering a special discount on the product. Not only do you want to offer a special discount on the product, but the product has to be priced below the price of the initial purchase that the customer has made.

If the customer has purchased a sweater for $50 and now you want to sell a second sweater as a backend sale, the second sweater needs to be priced below $50. Now that might be obvious because you're selling a second product at a discount price, but let's say that type of sweater is not the same type of sweater that the customer has bought. Let's say the customer has bought a 100% cotton sweater and now you want to offer the customer a wool sweater and the wool sweater is a different design, a different style, a different color, so it's not a second of the same type of an item. Sure it's a sweater, but it's a different type of a sweater. In this type of situation, you need to make sure that the wool sweater that you are selling is priced at least 50% below the price of the first sweater. In that case since you sold the first sweater for $50, the second sweater needs to be sold at $25 or less. This way the customer will feel that not only are you offering him a really good buy and a really good product with plenty of benefits and a product that's complimentary or similarly related to what he has first bought, but that you're also offering the product at a substantial savings. By offering the product at a substantial savings, the customer will know that he is really being rewarded for being a good customer and that he is being rewarded for making a purchase, and he is able to benefit from being a customer by having an instant opportunity to purchase a secondary product at a good discount.

Whatever the backend sale is that you have, whether it's for a product or a service, you always need to make sure that the backend sale is priced at least 50% less than the price of the initial product or service that was purchased by the customer. The reason that you're doing this is because you want the customer to not have any hesitancy regarding the purchase. See the reason that the backend sale is so effective that you want to make it so pain free, you want the customer to feel that he is already buying from you and that the next offering that you're giving him is so cheap that it's so cheap compared to his first purchase and he is getting so much in comparison with what first spent that he might as well buy it because he might not have that opportunity again. If you can covey that feeling and that message to your customer through the backend sale, then your backend sale might actually be higher than the national statistic of 50% and you might actually end up selling a lot more to your customers. The backend sale is also a great way to make a customer feel appreciated. It's even better sometimes than giving a customer something for free.

When you give a customer something for free, usually what you're giving the customer is something of a small value and the customer and the customer realizes that there is not that much value and that is why you are giving it away for free. But if you go ahead and give the customer something that really has a lot of value and you give that offering to the customer at a substantial savings then the customer will fully appreciate it and will feel glad that he is doing business with you.

Backend sales are a great way to increase customer loyalty and to increase revenue. Millionaire business owners use backend sales for loyalty-building forums, to build long-term customer relationships, and to increase their revenues through having increased sales opportunities.

11

Millionaire business owners know that in order for them to be able to grow their businesses they not only need to focus on customer acquisition and on further increasing the level of sales that they have and the levels of revenues and profits that they have, but they know that they need to also focus on their ability to spend money to grow their businesses. Millionaire business owners are never afraid to spend money on their business when they know that spending money on their business is going to help them expand their business and take their business to the next level. You see a millionaire business owner knows that in order for his or her business to be successful, it will require having to spend money in the business.

Most entrepreneurs make a mistake in this regard because while they are willing to spend money in their business, they're not always willing to take the next step and to risk more than they initially were planning on in the pursuit of their business. You see millionaire business owners will very often take money out of their own pockets and invest it into their business even when they're business is only producing a certain amount of revenue and even if those revenues are enough to cover the expenses of the business and to give them a decent profit, they'll sometimes reinvest those profits and take additional money out of their pocket to continue growing their business.

The choice that differentiates millionaire business owners from regular entrepreneurs and other small business owners is that millionaire business owners are willing to spend money out of their own pockets in their business even when their business is already producing a profit. But most entrepreneurs and small business owners will only be willing to spend money in their business that's generated by their business. For example, an entrepreneur who has a business producing a $5000 a month profit will be willing to spend that $5000 a month profit to reinvest in the business by either spending more money in advertising and marketing, on buying more merchandise, on hiring an employee, on expanding the size of the business, but what a millionaire business owner will do is besides the $5000 profit that's being generated on a monthly basis, the millionaire business owner will take money out of his or her pocket to expand the business. This differentiation in philosophy is what helps a millionaire business owner actually reach the next level of business.

Another differentiating factor between a millionaire business owner and a regular business owner when it comes to spending money is that the millionaire business owner knows that there's a direct correlation between spending money in his business and the level of success that his business will attain. For example, a millionaire business owner knows that the more money that he spends I advertising, the more customers will see his ads, the more customers will be exposed to his advertising message, and the more customers will be able to respond to his advertising. You see, a regular business owner will say "I only have $500 a month to which I can devote to advertising and I'll look to benefit from the result of that $500 worth of advertising, but I'll always limit the advertising level to that amount.

A millionaire business owner will continuously increase the amount of money that they're spending on advertising because they know that the more that they advertise, proportionately, the more results that they will produce. Millionaire business owners look at advertising and marketing as the lifeblood of their business because that is the process by which they will able to bring in more customers and encourage more customers to make purchases from them. So what they do is to not overspend on advertising by always making sure that they get the best bargain in advertising, they always continuously negotiate prices when it comes to advertising so that they can be sure they are paying the least amount of money for the advertising that they're receiving. But on the other hand, if they can obtain a great deal on their advertising, they're going to be willing to spend the money on it.

For example, if they have an opportunity to reach a circulation of 500,000 people through a magazine that's specifically tailored toward their market, they're going to be willing to spend whatever takes to have a good advertisement in that publication so that they can reach their market. You see, they're not always expense-oriented, meaning that even though they want to save on the amount of money that they're spending on advertising and they want to get the best rate for their advertising, when they see an opportunity to market their product successfully and to advertise efficiently, they're going to be willing to spend that money.

If there are two publications and one publication reaches 50,000 readers and another publication reaches 100,000 readers, if the publication that reaches 50,000 readers costs $50 but the publication that reaches 100,000 readers costs $75, they will spend the $75 so that they can reach those extra 50,000 readers. And now there is an entrepreneur, an entrepreneur who is just starting out in business will sometimes make the mistake of saying "Look you know what, for $50 I can reach 50,000 and that's a good enough market, so let me spread it out, let me advertise over there and as time goes on I'll upgrade my advertising." A millionaire business owner will feel confident and will go ahead and spend the $75 in advertising because it means that he'll be able to reach a much larger market base. See the millionaire business owner is not someone who's not throwing out money, meaning before he or she actually spends any money on advertising he or she has already consulted different trial runs. They've already taken out small runs or small ads in different small circulation publications that cost them only a minimal amount of money. When they are able to assess the results of their advertising and their marketing campaigns, then they can determine if their marketing campaigns are effective and if they work. Once they determine that their advertising campaigns do work, then they're not going to have an issue with spending more money to reach a higher circulation base.

Millionaire business owners also know that it's not just how much money they spend for their advertisement but what it is that they're getting for their advertisement. If one publication will allow them for the same price to reach their customers in a much more efficient way, either by giving them a larger display ad or allowing them to have colors in their advertisement, if the price is the same they will of course choose to have the ad that has more features and benefits to it. On the other hand, they will also spend more money for an ad that has more features and benefits if that ad will be able to solicit more customers for them and will be able to produce more inquiries into the products and services that they are selling.

Another way that millionaire business owners are willing to spend more money is if they have a retail location that depends on traffic. In order to have business, they will choose to pay a higher rent to have a higher traffic location as opposed to having a location that has less traffic and is less expensive. A millionaire business owner would rather be in a high traffic location that's more expensive because he knows that the more customers they have that see their retail establishment will mean the more customers that they will have coming into their retail establishment which will lead to having more sales.

Many people who open a retail location, especially when it's the first retail location that they're opening will make the mistake of starting out in a very conservative fashion. They'll say to themselves "Let me take a store that cost only $800-$900 a month to run, even though they know that store has less of a foot traffic that will be able to pass by my store, that way I'll be able to see how my business does." They figure that they're satisfied with having a lower level of income as long as the risk that they're taking is also lower. A millionaire business owner will only role out their business and will only lease a retail location once they've done their research, once they have obtained expert advice, and once they have tested out the product and service that they're going to be offering so that they feel comfortable in taking a much larger risk. This way they can know that when they take this much larger risk they're also going to be able to benefit by having a much larger marketplace from which they can make money. They don't view the extra expense as a risk; they view the extra expense as the ability to make more money for their business. They know that the more money that they spend on their business it will produce a higher level of income for their business.

A millionaire business owner would rather spend $5000 a month rent on a high-traffic location that can produce a gross revenue of $20,000-$30,000 a month than to have a location that has less traffic that only costs $1000 a month and that retail location can only produce revenues of $2000-$3000 a month. You see, in the retail world, usually a high-traffic location that costs more money to rent, will have an exponential advantage than a location that has less traffic and it will also cost less to rent.

Millionaire business owners know that the more money that they spend in their business, as long as they have researched their decisions and their decisions are well thought out from a business and a strategic point of view, that it will also mean that there will be a direct correlation between the amount of money that they're spending and those decisions that they're making will bring into the business. Millionaire business owners know that the spending money in their business is important because in order for the business person to succeed that the business person always needs to have something to sell whether it's a product or a service that they're selling. In order to have that product or service, they need to spend money on it. If you want to look at it this way, think about buying merchandise. The more merchandise you're able to buy, the larger of a discount you can get for that merchandise. Many people make the mistake of not taking full advantage of all the discounts that they can get because they don't want to overstock themselves with merchandise, but this is a mistake.

If you have thought out the kind of merchandise that you are going to be selling or the type of service that you are going to be offering, you know that there is a market for the product or service that you're offering. You know that you are selling the product or service at a good price, and knowing that, you should be able to spend money on stocking your business, even if you have to overstock it. If you spend $1000 on merchandise for which you are able to get a 10% discount and then you spend $3000 on merchandise for which you are able to get a 20% discount, you're better off spending that $3000 on merchandise and getting that 20% discount, even if it's going to take you three times as long to sell all of your merchandise. You see it doesn't make a difference whether you buy a $1000 worth of merchandise and sell that merchandise in one month or you buy $3000 worth of merchandise and sell that merchandise over the course of three months. Either way, if you're in business for the long-term, you are going to need merchandise for the next three months, so why not spend money now and buy all of the merchandise that you'll need for the next three months? You'll get a larger discount for the merchandise and then you'll make more money as you sell the merchandise over the course of the next three months. If you buy $3000 worth of merchandise and receive a 20% discount, you're making an extra 10% on the merchandise as opposed to if you purchase a $1000 worth of merchandise each month and receive the 10% discount on the merchandise.

The millionaire business owner looks to take every discount available and sometimes buy all of the merchandise that they will need for the coming year because they know that they have a good market for the merchandise, they know at what price they can sell it, they know that they're offering a high-quality item or a high-quality service for which there is a strong existing market demand. They don't mind stocking their businesses at the beginning of the year because they know that over the next twelve months they will be able to sell everything that they have currently purchased. The millionaire business owner has the mindset that he would rather get every possible discount that he can obtain now; even if it means that he's stocking his business with merchandise.

Let's say for instance that you buy $10,000 worth of merchandise at the beginning of the year and that it will take you a full twelve months to sell that merchandise, but at the end of the twelve months you'll have sold that merchandise for $50,000. Now your profit is $40,000, and that's not bad. Let's look at the example in another way, let's say that every month you had bought not $10,000 worth of merchandise, but had bought only $1000 worth of merchandise. In buying your merchandise that way because you were not able to maximize your savings and take advantage of the discounts offered to large volume purchasers, at the end of the year that $12,000 worth of merchandise only turned into $30,000. The other way, if you have initially spent $12,000 up front on merchandise, that turned into $40,000 because you were able to buy more merchandise because you were able to take advantage of the discount. You can look at it two ways, on one hand you're saving money, you don't have to spend as much money because you're seeing a higher discount on the merchandise and the extra money that you would have had to spend otherwise can be kept in your pocket, used to pay your credit card bills, used to go on a vacation, used to buy clothing, used to make your mortgage payment, or you can use the discount to buy more merchandise. If you only have

$2000 to buy merchandise, but now you're able to get a 10% discount, which means that for the $2000 you'll be able to actually buy $2200 worth of merchandise. If you're able to double your money on that merchandise, that $2200 worth of merchandise will now be worth $4400. So you've actually taken that $2000 and turned it into $4400. If you had not taken advantage of that 10% discount then the $2000 that you're spending on merchandise would have only become $4000 and you would have given up a $400 profit because you didn't take advantage of every discount that was available.

Millionaire business owners always inquire of their suppliers and of their landlords what they can do to obtain the best discounts whether they're purchasing a product, whether they're purchasing a service such as accounting work, legal work, or consulting work. They ask their landlords for every type of discount that they can receive, whether it's reducing the amount of rent they pay, reducing their mortgage payments, or whether it's obtaining better terms in their lease agreements.

Millionaire business owners will offer to prepay rent in order to save money on the amount of money which they are paying. They are very savvy in looking for every opportunity to spend money. They proactively offer to spend more money in order to receive a better discount. This is a great negotiating technique because they can approach their suppliers and advise them that they can either wait five months to make $5000 from them or they will give them $5000 right now and they won't have to wait the five months that would otherwise have to wait. But for that $5000, they don't want to receive $5000 worth of merchandise, but they want to receive $6000 or $7000 worth of merchandise. The supplier will be tempted to agree with this offer because even though he will be making less money on the merchandise that he's selling to the millionaire business owner but he would rather have all of the money upfront so that he can invest it into his own business and so that he can enjoy the money that it would otherwise take him five months to make.

You can apply the strategy that millionaire business owners use on a small scale or a large scale. You don't have to yet be at the stage where you can spend thousands of dollars on merchandise in order to benefit from this strategy. You can emulate millionaire business owners even if you only spend a few hundred dollars on merchandise every month. You can approach your supplier and tell him that instead of spending $100 on purchasing supplies for your store that you are willing to spend $200 but you want to receive a better discount. If you are receiving credit from a supplier, ask the supplier what kind of a discount he would give you if you prepay or if you pay before your bills are due. There are many companies that will offer a 2% discount on their invoices if you pay for those invoices before the due date or if you pay within fifteen days of receiving the invoice. You can negotiate a higher discount if you decide to forego credit and pay upfront for all your purchases.

While millionaire business owners are very careful about the money that they spend, they do have a willingness to spend money and they're very creative in negotiating situations in which they can gain volume discounts, gain service discounts, or gain additional services and products as they spend more money. They also always have money in reserve so that when they see an opportunity, they can jump on that opportunity and make money from that opportunity before them. What millionaire business owners never to is to never hesitate to spend money in their business and they're sure that by spending money they can make more money in their business. See many people pass up great opportunities only because they're not comfortable spending money in their business or because they feel uncomfortable with the level of income that they're business is producing. Millionaire business owners reach their status of wealth because every time they see an opportunity to make money they act on that opportunity.

Millionaire business owners know that there is no guarantee that they will see any future opportunities from which they can make money, so while they do have opportunities to make money they act upon those opportunities and do whatever is required in order to make money. For example, if they see a special closeout offer to buy 100 pairs of sneakers at $3.00 a pair, they will jump on that opportunity because they know that these sneakers regularly wholesale for $20 a pair and there are no assurances that they will ever see these sneakers offered to them again at this price or even at a price below the regular wholesale cost.

Millionaire business owners realize when they spend money that they never know in the beginning exactly how that opportunity will end up resulting. When they see an opportunity to make money they act upon it quickly because they realize that if they market the opportunity themselves, they might make even more money than they originally thought they would make or even more money than the seller on the other side who is involved in this transaction thinks that they can make. If the millionaire business owner sees a small property that's being marketed by a real estate broker, the millionaire business owner realizes that a real estate broker might not have the same creativity or the same access to marketing strategy that the millionaire business owner, so the millionaire business owner will be willing to spend the money to buy that property because he or she knows that they have a much better marketing strategy to sell this house and a much better opportunity to sell this house.

The same ideas should be applied to any business regardless of the size of the business. If there's an opportunity to make money, an entrepreneur needs to realize that there is no assurance that the opportunity to make money will be repeated and that this could be the opportunity of a lifetime and if you want your business to continue growing and you want to make as much money as possible, you need to act upon every opportunity that you see; provided you research the opportunity beforehand and you know that there is a strong demand for that opportunity.

Millionaire business owners also know that it's important to spend money on equipment that they need in order to operate their business. Millionaire business owners will not hesitate spending more money on a better computer that will help them to make more money in their business. Millionaire business owners will not hesitate to spend money on renting a truck, or leasing an automobile, on buying the correct clothing, on renting a good office, on having good office furniture, as long as all of these components are specifically related towards their making money in their business and towards increasing their level of business. In order for you to be able to understand why all of these concepts are beneficial, you need to start putting some of these concepts into action. Until you put these concepts into action yourself, you will not be able to see how valuable these ideas are and why millionaire business owners attribute so much of their success to these concepts including the concept of always being willing to spend money on your business as long as spending money on that business will produce direct financial benefits to your venture.

12

Millionaire business owners know that in order to succeed in business they're going to need to count on a constant stream of customers. They're going to need to have a steady flow of customers in order to increase their revenues and in order to maintain their customer base due to expected loss of customers due to attrition or due to some of their customers exiting the business or due to some of their customers moving on to doing business with some of their competitors.

Since millionaire business owners know that in order for them to succeed they'll always need to have a growing base of customers, they have two options. One option is that they can do a heavy amount of marketing and advertising which will help to bring in customers. They can hope that the advertising and marketing that they're doing brings in enough customers while not proving to be too expensive to the point where it eliminates a large portion or most of their profits.

Another way that savvy millionaire business owners are able to bring in a constant flow of customers without having to spend any money of their own is through the power of referrals. Referrals, and we'll now call this "referral marketing" is a process that by using all your contacts, and the people to whom your contacts introduce you, to supply you with a steady number of customers. You see referral is the perfect method of soliciting new customers because it does two of the following things. One, it eliminates the need to spend money on advertising. If you have a steady amount of customers coming in through referrals, you don't have to spend the money that you would otherwise need to spend to bring in those customers.

Now while you still want to spend money to advertise and market your business so that you're brining in customers, you will be able to reach a point through your application of referral marketing that you will never have to spend any money on conducting any advertising. If you're able to continue growing your business through the process of referral marketing, you'll get to that point pretty soon where you won't have to spend money in advertising because you'll have enough people referring customers to you and have a system in place where you're constantly obtaining new leads of people without having to spend any money on soliciting new business.

Referral marketing also accomplishes something else. Besides eliminating the need to spend large sums of money on advertising and marketing, you are able to bring in new business which will perceive you very differently than the other business that you bring in through your advertising and marketing campaigns.

Let me give you an example. If you place an advertisement in your local newspaper and that advertisement produces thirty or forty good solid inquiries, now those people who call you in response to your advertisement are interested in the product or the service that you're offering enough to want to call and get further information. The big dilemma that you are still going to encounter is that you will have to overcome the credibility factor. You're going to have to get to a point where your customers feel comfortable with you where these people trust you to pay you for your services or products.

Remember, at this point besides your advertisement, you're still a stranger to them and they're not familiar with you or your business. On the other hand, when you solicit a new lead through referral marketing, the person feels comfortable doing business with you to some extent because they've been referred by either a friend or a close associate. That referral was only produced because the person who referred them to you already had a relationship with you, whether it is a social relationship or a business relationship, they already have a relationship with you which allows them to feel comfortable in wanting to do business with you and which allows them to feel comfortable enough to want to contact you and to want to give your business a chance.

Referral marketing gives you instant credibility. Think about the credibility you receive when a relative whose been doing business with you for ten years lets another one of their relatives know about your business. When that relative walks into the door, since they have a relative who's already been doing business with you, they'll feel comfortable in completing a transaction with you. The same happens in the service business. Most doctors and attorneys get most of their business through referrals. The reason that this is true is because if someone has used their legal services or their medical services and they feel very comfortable with using this professional, when they then let someone else know about the services that they're referring from this attorney or this doctor, then those people will feel very comfortable in doing business with them. When people use an attorney, it's usually for a very important matter about which they don't want to take any chance and they want to make sure that there is no room for errors. When you're using that attorney or that doctor, you always want to make sure that you're not going to make a mistake and that the person giving you that legal advice or the person giving you those medical services is a competent professional who can help you can guide you through the process by giving you good advice and of helping you with whatever issue you're dealing and with whatever challenges that need to be overcome.

So who else would you rather trust than someone who you know who has already been providing services through a close relative of yours, through a friend, or through a business associate? In other words, if you're about to undergo surgery and before you get that surgery you want to make sure that this doctor is competent, that this doctor is good and that when he does a surgery he has a high level of surgical skills. The best way to know that this doctor knows what he's doing is by speaking to someone who has already used this doctor's services. If you speak to another patient of his and you know that the patient is satisfied with his or her services, then you'll also feel comfortable in using that doctor for services. Now there are two ways in which you could go about finding that doctor. You can make inquiries on your own and hope to speak to people and ask them whom they have used when they have needed a doctor and whom they have used when they have needed an attorney.

The same is true the other way around. If the doctor or an attorney wants to set up some business, they should speak to their recurring clients and ask them who else might be in need of their services. The way that a doctor or an attorney, or for that matter any savvy business person can attract a good steady amount of customers is by always making it a habit of asking all of their current customers and their current clients who else might need their services and asking them for the names of any people whom you can contact to discuss your services.

Let me give you an example. Let's say that you have a furniture business and your business supplies furniture to newlyweds. Your furniture business could also consist of supplying furniture for babies and children. The best way for you to have solid leads is to speak to the people who are already buying from you. If a family comes to you and buys furniture from you and they're happy with what they've bought, they're happy with the quality of furniture, the colors of the furniture, the furniture is of good quality that will last a long time, and they've had no problems with it, they won't have a problem referring you to other people. The reason that family would be the best source of referrals for you is because a family or in the case of a newlywed couple, by nature people socialize with people who are in similar circumstances and come from backgrounds similar to their own. So a newlywed couple will have within their social circles other newlywed couples and then they can refer you to other newlywed couples who are in the process of shopping for furniture. What you should do each time you sell to a newlywed couple or even if you meet with a newlywed couple, ask them if they wouldn't mind writing down the names of three or four people who could benefit from the services or products that you provide.

In the example of the newlywed couple, if they are your customers and they come into your furniture store and they purchase furniture from you, when you give them a follow up call a week later to see if they're satisfied with what they've purchased from you and inquire if there's anything else that you can provide for them, ask them at the same time if they know of any couples who could benefit from the furniture that you sell. Ask them if they would be comfortable in giving you the names or three or four people, and after they give you the names of those three or four people, then ask them to call those people and let them to know to expect a call from you.

Most people who are happy doing business with you and if they like you will feel extremely comfortable doing so because they'll feel that it's a way to pay you back for having gone the extra mile to make sure that they were satisfied. See most people are not used to receiving a follow up call after they've done business with someone. Most people realize that once they've purchased the merchandise or paid for the service which they've received that the people who sold them that product or service usually will move on to concentrate on new customers. It would be so unexpected on their part if they receive a phone call inquiring whether they are satisfied with the service or product that they have received. When you make a good impression with people, they will feel that you are happy with what it is that you're providing, then they will go out of their way to also see how they can help you grow your business.

You can also take this a step further and not only wait for business from referrals to whom you've already sold, but you can also go ahead and speak to people with whom you are meeting for the first time. Many times people genuinely will not need your product or service, even though they do enjoy dealing with you and even though they do see the need for what it is that you are offering. You see, every time a customer says "No", you shouldn't take that to mean that they don't want what you're offering or that they don't need what you're offering, but you should also realize that they could be in a situation where the customer really initially was interested in buying your product or service but after discussing the matter with his wife or discussing it with his business partner, he came to the conclusion that he just does not have the money at this time to spend on what you're offering. But if he felt comfortable in the way that you dealt with him and he felt that you were a real professional and were very knowledgeable about the subject which you were discussing with him, he should not have a problem in referring people to you. He might actually want to refer people to you because he'll appreciate that you've taken the time to explain everything that you're offering to him and that you've spent the time dealing with him, and that you are a professional, especially if you did come across as a knowledgeable professional in the business area in which you are involved, he'll want to refer people to you. He'll want the people with whom he deals to be able to benefit from your services.

What you can do in this situation is after the person has expressed that he is not interested in your offer, or even if the person is unsure as to whether they're interested, during that first meeting with the person, when the meeting is complete, take out a notebook and a pen and ask that person for the names and phone numbers of five people who he thinks can benefit from what you are offering. If you do this, in a very short period of time, you'll have more leads than you can handle.

Let me give you an example. Let's say that on an average, your first week you meet with twenty potential customers, for instance you're an insurance broker who meets with twenty people who might be interested in the service which you offer. You ask each of those twenty people for five leads, most people will have no problem giving you the names and numbers of five people. Some of the people might ask that you not tell that lead that they gave you the name because they're a coworker of theirs or a business associate of theirs, but usually people will have no problem giving you the leads whether they're relatives of theirs, friends of theirs, business associates of theirs, or whether they're coworkers. If you meet with twenty people your first week and each of those twenty people give you five leads, you're going to have 100 leads to call on the next week.

Now think about how much time you'll need to contact those 100 leads. If you want to contact all those people the first week, you're going to have to contact at least thirteen people a day so that you can see everyone that you can see during your first week. When you go to meet all those people, let's see all the benefits that the referral process can bring to you. Millionaire business owners know that this referral marketing process is extremely lucrative for the following reasons: it brings in a steady number of leads, it generates exposure to the customers that they'll want to see and that exposure leads also to an eventual increase in business.

If you have twenty customers your first week and even if none of those customers initially purchase from you, if each of those customers give you five leads which amounts to one 100 leads, if you'll contact those 100 leads during the next week, out of those 100 people you contact, you only add 20% of those people decide to become customers, that's now 20 customers more than what you had. If each of those 100 people that you see gives you 5 leads, then you now have 500 leads to contact. If 10% of those people decide to become your customers, there are 50 customers plus the initial ten customers from the first 100 leads, now that's 60 customers with whom you're dealing. If you now get five from each of those 500 people you contact, you now have 2500 leads and if 10% of those people decide to become customers now you'll have approximately 250 customers, plus the first 60 customers that you had from the beginning, so that's 310 customers. All this can be done in three weeks if you're very aggressive in soliciting referrals from all the people with whom you do business.

Remember it's not just the 310 customers that you have now, but think about how many more leads those customer will be giving you in the future. Someone might only have a lead for you on Monday, but when they come in next week, they might have two leads for you and then three months later they might meet someone who's a good potential customer for you and he could provide you that person's name as another lead. So if you have a total of 100 good customers, those customers can provide leads for you every month. You can contact all your customers once a month and ask them if they can give you the names of five new people whom you can contact. Even if each of those customers only gives you two new names every month, that's 200 new names a month, or 2400 names a year. If out of those 2400 names a year you turn 10% of those people into customers, that's 240 customers, if you turn 20% of those people into customers, that's 480 customers. If your average profit per customer is $100 and you have 480 customers, that's $48,000, but you don't have to stop there. Remember you are not working with customers for the short term.

Millionaire business owners know that the value of a customer, as we discussed earlier is the lifetime value of that customer. If on average every customer makes five purchase a year from you, five purchases times $100 is $500, we still have 480 customers, so now that's now $240,000 a year which wouldn't require you to do any advertising or marketing on your own. All of those customers resulted from your meeting with your current customers, speaking to them and soliciting new leads from them, and from aggressively marketing your business through referral marketing. You see the benefits of referral marketing are almost endless. Every time you bring a new customer in, that customer will not just give you leads when you first bring him in as a customer, but can give you leads through your lifetime relationship with that customer.

The same is true for people you know on a social or a business basis. People who are your customers who enjoy doing business with you or who just enjoy your company will feel comfortable continuously introducing you to people whom they feel could benefit from doing business with you. Referral marketing also helps you on the supplier side. If you need to hire good sources for products or you need to hire good employees or you want to find good independent sales representatives who can go ahead and sell the merchandise that you have or sell the services that you are offering, through referral marketing you can obtain the names and leads for good supplier of what it is that you are offering or good independent sales reps or good employees.

For instance, if you're purchasing socks from a certain manufacturer and now you want to purchase briefs, your current manufacturer might not manufacture briefs, but you can ask that manufacturer who makes socks whom he knows in the business who manufactures briefs. If he doesn't know of someone who manufactures briefs, he can probably introduce you to someone who can help you find out who manufactures briefs. The manufacturer of the socks wants to keep his good customer and will know that if he gives you good sales leads or good supplies leads as in this case that you will in turn give him different sales leads which can help him grow his business.

As long as you set up a system where you're continuously exchanging your referrals with your customers, suppliers, associates, colleagues, lawyers, doctors, accountants, or other service professionals, you'll be in a situation where you'll be continuously receiving sales leads, supplier leads, or any type of leads that you need. You'll be in a situation where people will want to give you leads and in which people will always be on the lookout for leads for you because they know that you will be supplying them with leads that they can use in their business.

Remember everything in life has to be a win-win situation. If you want to be able to continuously receive good leads, you need to be able to supply good leads. The way that you do that is to actively stay involved with your business and by actively helping other people with their business needs. If you keep this in mind then your referral marketing strategy can be very successful and in no time you will be able to find yourself in a situation in which millionaire business owners find themselves when they can count on 80% of their customers to come in through referrals.

Millionaire business owners also make sure to continuously reward the people who give them referrals. If it's permitted in your industry you should go about compensating people through a small commission for any business that they refer to you. If it's not permitted in your business to compensate people for referrals, such as in the life insurance business or the financial industry, then you should compensate people in the way in which you are allowed. Maybe you could compensate them by giving them a gift card, giving them tickets to a Broadway show, or through deep gratitude which you are going to express by asking them how you can help them grow their business and how you can help them. Maybe you could put them in contact with people who have something to offer them.

There should always be a way for you to help people grow their business and there's always something that you can offer people to help them whether or not they're in business. You could help people find a good deal on a vacation home, you could help people find a book for which they are looking, you could help people by introducing them to other people on a business or a social basis, but regardless of what you do, remember that people do enjoy feeling appreciated and one of the best ways that you can show people that you appreciate them is by actually offering them something in exchange for what they are giving you.

Remember people don't do things just because they want to receive something, but it's just a nice, decent practice on your part to find ways to practically thank people for the help that they are giving you like providing you with referrals. If you get into the habit of expressing this gratitude towards people, they will go out of their way to help you grow your business by giving you referrals.

Millionaire business owners know that in order to succeed in business they're going to have to resort to innovative strategies that can help them grow their business and those strategies, if they can draw upon the resources of other parties then they can use those resources to be able to make up for some of their weaknesses. In other words, millionaire business owners are always on the lookout for joint venture opportunities that could help both parties make money and that could bring benefits to all of the parties based upon each party's respective trends which will help cover the other party's weakness by using the benefits that both parties bring into the picture to make money for both parties.

Millionaire business owners look for joint venture opportunities that will expose them to new markets that will help to expose them to the market base that they want to reach by being able to draw upon the marketing skills or the sales skills of the other party. Sometimes when there are business that are both looking for certain results, even though both businesses don't operate in each other's marketplace and they each have a different set of customers, because of the nature of each of their respective customers, they see an opportunity to make money by cross-marketing to each other's customers. Millionaire business owners look for joint ventures where the opportunity will not only make them money now, but ones that can be set up as long-term opportunities where both parties can continue making money. They look for joint venture opportunities that will require that they spend little or no money upfront that will give a strong incentive to their partner in the venture, so the partner will want to stay in for the long-term. They also know that the joint venture opportunity, even though it can be very lucrative, can have certain pitfalls so they have to be very careful. When they construct this joint venture, they want to make sure that the other party does not tarnish their image. They want to make sure that whatever party with whom they're associated has very high ethical and moral standards so that their products or services will not be marketed through an unethical strategy which could backfire on their other business interest. When they conduct their business, millionaire business owners know that the impression they make upon their customers can last a lifetime, so they're very careful with whom they form joint ventures because they know that their reputation is very important. They don't want to be involved with a venture partner who even if it is a venture partner who doesn't market their venture in an immoral or unethical way that venture partner is not associated with any business that is unethical or immoral in its practices. People will associate that partner, even if that partner is not involved in the other business, with immoral or unethical activity. When you see a company like IBM marketing AT&T's Long Distance Services for Small Businesses, IBM will make sure that AT&T is a company that has very high ethical and moral standards. If AT&T should later on do something that is unethical, IBM does not want to be associated with that unethical perception. People will only remember that once upon a time, IBM was marketing AT&T's services and that AT&T got into trouble so maybe there was something wrong with IBM all along and that it is using the same practices that got AT&T into trouble. Of course we all know that both IBM and AT&T are great companies and neither company has been in trouble, they're both good, reputable companies and that's why companies like IBM and AT&T like to form joint ventures.

For the same reason, millionaire business owners look to form joint ventures with other businesses in the market which can help them reach the customers that they want to reach or can help them expand into other areas wherein they can make money. If a joint venture partner has a product or a service that is complimentary to what you're offering, then they look to be of value to them because they know that they can either market the product or service from their joint venture partner as a backend sale or as add-on to what it is that they are selling.

For example, a clothing company that has retail outlet throughout New York State, which focuses on men's suits will want to form a joint venture with a chain of dry cleaners. The owner of the suit store will also want to offer his customers a 10% discount on the services of a dry cleaner. Now that joint venture is good for the dry cleaner and it's good for the national retailer. It's good for the national retailer because the customer will want to buy the suit since they'll know that after buying the suit, the first dry-cleaning that they have to purchase for their suit will be at a 10% discount. The dry-cleaner will be very happy because he will receive a lot of business from all of the customers that purchase suits from this national retailer because at some point those customers will have to get their suits cleaned. The joint venture in this case doesn't require any money from either party; the only marketing costs are the expense of the national retailer advertising the fact that his customers can receive a 10% discount on their first dry-cleaning service for their suits. The reason that advertising is really not expensive and the reason why it doesn't have to be perceived as an additional cost is because the national suit retailer is already spending money on advertising and marketing. Now it only needs to add an additional line that that advertising and marketing indicating to its customers their offer of a 10% discount on dry-cleaning services for their customers who purchase suits from them. The owner of the dry-cleaning chain is very happy because even though he has to give up 10% of the revenues that come in from the dry-cleaning of suits, he will have a lot more customers who purchase dry-cleaning services for their suits. Let's say that this discount dry-cleaner on a national basis receives 100,000 customers per week. Even though it's going to be reducing its revenues by 10%, it is only going to be reducing its revenues by 10% on people who have purchased their suits from the national suit retailer. And even in that case, when it is receiving 10% less from those customers, it is actually increasing its revenues from those customers by 90% because otherwise it would never have had those customers in the first place. These are customers who are only coming to this dry-cleaner because they have purchased a suit from this specific suit retailer and they know now that they can receive a 10% discount from this dry-cleaner. That is why they will go to this dry-cleaner, in order to receive that 10% discount whenever they need their suit cleaned. Both the national suit retailer and the national dry-cleaner are both happy to engage in this joint venture.

There's also another reason why they're both going to be happy about being involved in this joint venture. As part of the joint venture, if both parties include in their literature and in their advertising the benefits that people can receive from doing business with them, then they'll attract a lot more business from people. Let's look at it this way. The suit retailer will be advertising the fact that all of its customers can receive a 10% discount at a certain dry-cleaning retail chain.

Now anyone who looks at that advertisement, whether or not buy a suit, is now going to be exposed to the dry-cleaner about whom they would not otherwise have known. If they are accustomed to using the dry-cleaning services of a competitor, now they will consider using the dry-cleaning services provided by this dry-cleaning service which has been advertised by the national suit retailer. It also works the other way. Anyone who walks into this dry-cleaning establishment and sees an advertisement there saying that anyone who purchases a suit from this certain retail chain will receive a 10% discount on dry-cleaning for that suit, will also be exposed to that national retail chain. Both parties who are involved in a joint venture or let the people know about the joint venture then people will be exposed to each partner, whether or not they previously knew about the partner. The party that's involved in the joint venture is having its name and its services advertised by the other party, just by virtue of both parties being involved in this joint venture. This means that both partners will be cognizant that each other's involved in this joint venture in order to gain customers and business directly from this joint venture, but also to draw upon the advertising and marketing ability of each of those parties.

We can also examine this concept on a very small scale. Let's say there's a small grocery store in your neighborhood and that you're opening a video store in your neighborhood. Now what you can do is enter into an agreement with the owner of the grocery store and tell them that every purchase someone makes by them that you are going to give those customers a coupon for 5% off which they can use at your video store. In exchange, you will give all the customers at your video store a 5% discount that they can use when they go to the grocery store. This will send customers from the grocery store to your video store and customers from your video store to the grocery store. Neither of these two businesses is competitive, so you wouldn't mind sending some of your customers to the grocery store and the grocery store wouldn't mind sending some of its customers to the video store.

Now as part of this joint venture you both will put a sign in your stores letting customers know what one of the benefits of making a purchase from you or a service from you. The benefit that you're offering is that once someone makes a purchase from you, you're enabling them to save 5% when they shop at this grocery store or you're enabling them to save 5% when they shop at the video store. If they don't make a purchase at the grocery store and if they don't make a purchase at the video store, they won't be able to take advantage of that 5%, or 10% or 15% discount at the other business. People might make a purchase just because they want to be able to receive the discount at the other business.

Think about it this way. At some point, everyone needs to buy groceries, but now it's a matter of where they would like to buy those groceries. Everyone knows that they need to buy milk every week, but it's up to them to decide where they want to buy their milk. They can buy the milk at a supermarket or they can buy the milk at any of the grocery stores in their neighborhood. If you want to draw people to a specific grocery store, then you would want people to know that when the make a purchase from that certain grocery store that they receive additional benefits besides the merchandise that they're buying. Those additional benefits are the discounts that they can now use at another establishment. So when a person walks into that grocery store and they're really not sure that they want to buy their milk over there because they're not really sure if the best prices are being offered here or they're just accustomed to buying their groceries from another grocery store. Then they see a sign on the wall which reads "All customers who purchase their groceries here receive a 5% discount on purchases at the local video store", then those customers might feel interested in making those purchases there so that they'll be able to save 5% on their video rentals.

Another benefit is that customers of that grocery store are in the habit of renting videos once a week, but they're used to renting their videos from your competitor and you want to draw those customers away from your competitor to your video store. What you would do is advertise and market your video store by allowing the customers of that grocery store to save 5% on their video rentals at your store. In this fashion you are bringing in customers from a grocery store who would instead be shopping at a video store other than yours. Most customers would say "Now, I can get a discount by going to this video store and it really doesn't matter where I rent the movie because they both have the same movies, but why should I go to the other video store when I can get a 5% discount to rent the video from this store and enjoy the same movie at a cheaper price?"

The same type of a joint venture opportunity can be used on any scale. You can go ahead and you can market joint venture services between a retail store, between a dentist, between an attorney and an accountant, an accountant and a CPA can market their services jointly, they can take out a large advertisement in the newspaper and list both of their names, but by taking a larger advertisement everyone will see their advertisement and more people will see that large advertisement than people would look at two different smaller advertisements. If you have a full-page ad in the newspaper, then people will look at your advertise-ment and see what in seeing what you're offering but also in what the other party is offering at the same time.

Let's say there are two different parties, there's an accountant and there's an attorney. The accountant, on his own can only afford to take a half-a-page advertisement in his local newspaper. That half-a-page advertisement will catch the attention of 5000 people. The attorney could also only afford to purchase a half-a-page advertisement in his local newspaper which will also only catch the attention of 5000 peo-ple. If they both combine their resources and split the cost of a full-page advertisement, then that full-page ad, since it is a full-page ad is more noticeable and will catch the attention of more people than two half-a-page ads. A large, full-page ad can actually catch the attention of 50,000 people or more. Not only will it catch the attention of more people, it can also provide additional benefits such as a credibility fac-

tor. If people see an attorney and a CPA take out a full-page advertisement in the newspaper, they'll see that these are serious people who
already have a lot of business because it takes a lot of business to be able
to take out a full-page ad in the newspaper, otherwise how could they
afford to take out a full-page ad in the newspaper? That full-page ad
also says to the consumer that this attorney and this CPA are both stak-
ing their reputations in marketing their services together, so both have
obviously verified each other's services and have a certain amount of
credibility because they are working together. People like to see an
attorney and a CPA working together and many other types of businesses working together because they view them as much more than a
fly-by-night operation when people see that those professional entities
that are working together. It gives people a perception of more
strength.

Millionaire business owners will always look for joint venture opportunities that will help them establish their creditability in the consumer's
perception. They will also look for joint venture opportunities that will
help them market themselves to a much larger market than they could
have otherwise afforded to do on their own. People who conduct these
joint venture opportunities are always on the lookout for partners who
will help enhance their reputation or will help enhance their offerings.
On the smaller scale, even if you're opening up a 99-Cent Store, you
can do this with a local restaurant. You can exchange coupons for each
other's business. Each time someone makes a purchase from you, you
put into their shopping bag a coupon for the restaurant business and
every time someone goes to the restaurant and receives their bill there
could be a coupon enclosed to shop at your 99-Cent Store. The restaurant will be happy because they'll be able to have customers who visit
your 99-Cent Store who will now be exposed to their restaurant and
you will be happy because people who go to your restaurant will now
be exposed to your 99-Cent Store and will now know about your business. When you do a joint venture opportunity, you'll be able to mar-

ket yourself towards people who might have known about you but had never tried out your services or products and will have a reminder in the form of a coupon which is a form of an advertisement and they'll consider trying out your services and products. You'll also have a lot more credibility in people's eyes and you'll also be able to reach a lot more people than you could have otherwise been able to reach in the first place.

Joint venture opportunities can also help both parties make money. They're not always just specifically for marketing products or services. Many times joint ventures work to actually put money in each other's pockets. Let's say you're the publisher of a newsletter and you have a newsletter that goes out to 10,000 subscribers. It's taken you a few years that build up this newsletter and your newsletter is on the topic of investing. You really like writing this newsletter, people respect it, and your readers look forward to receiving this newsletter every month. In the newsletter you have advertisements from different firms that want to advertise their financial services. For an average advertisement, you are being paid $200. For that $200, someone gets a ¼ page ad in your newsletter. If you have thirty or forty ads in your newsletter, we're talking about between $6000-$8000 a month which is a good income.

Let's say now that you want to take the earning level of that newsletter to the next step. You can contact the following parties to look for a joint venture opportunity you can use to deliver money into your pocket. You can contact a financial publisher who sells investment books and tell the publisher that you will give him a free advertisement in your newsletter. Tell him that your newsletter reaches 10,000 active investors who are interested in reading and learning about investing and that if he advertises his books through your publication you think that he'll end up selling a lot of books. In response, the customer will say that he appreciates your offer but that he gets so many offers to advertise his publications that he tries to only stick with publications of which he is familiar or at this point he just doesn't have the money to purchase any additional advertising. Your reply to the publisher will be that you are giving him a free advertisement at absolutely no cost to him. The only thing that you are asking is that for every book that he sells through your newsletter that you receive $5. If that publisher sells his books for $20, he'll have no problem giving you $5 per book, otherwise his cost to sell those books could either be through expensive advertisement or a 50% fee that he has to give up to a wholesaler of his book such as Amazon, Barnes & Nobles, or any wholesaler or person who distributes books.

You're giving the publisher an opportunity to publish books and to sell books through being able to have a way to advertise his books without having to market them. The way that you do that is to tell the publisher that he or she can receive 75% of the gross proceeds from the sale of the book since you're only asking for 25% or $5 in this case. The reason the publisher would want to do this is because the publisher wouldn't have to spend any money on advertising and the publisher doesn't have to give up a much larger percentage from the sale of the books as opposed to when he sells the books through a regular wholesaler or through retail channels. This opportunity is very lucrative for you because if you have 10,000 readers who feel comfortable with your publication and they like your publication and they view you as a reliable source of information, they will be interested in anything that you are promoting and especially anything that's being perceived as an endorsement by you. If you personally endorse a book that his publisher has for sale and you let the publisher of the book know that you are going to not only be advertising the book but that you are going to be writing an article about the book and will be telling your readers why you strongly recommend that they purchase this book, the publisher will see a much higher percentage of orders as opposed to an advertisement in a similar publication.

The reason is that people respond in certain ways to advertisements. They know that it's an advertisement and that someone is pushing that product or service and then it's up to them to decide whether they want it. But then again, anytime people see advertisements, their defenses are up and those advertisements have to overcome those defenses in order to make sales. When people see a product or service being personally endorsed by someone whom they respect and trust, they'll respond that much more favorably to that so-called advertisement. In this case if you personally endorse the book that the publisher has for sale through your newsletter, instead of receiving a 5% response rate, you can receive a 20%-30% response rate on what you are offering. That of course is a given so long as the product or service that you are promoting and endorsing is extremely similar to what you would otherwise be promoting and endorsing to your customers.

If you have an investment newsletter on helping retirees maintain their portfolio during their retirement years, then you would want to promote a book on investing specifically aimed towards retirees through your publication. This way the product that you are promoting and endorsing is extremely commensurate with the topic of your newsletter. If you do that, you can receive easily a 10%-15% response rate at minimum. If you have 10,000 subscribers to your newsletter and you receive a 15% response rate, that's 1500 orders. If you're receiving $5 for every book that's sold through your newsletter, you're talking about $7500 in your pocket. Think about that, an advertisement that you would have otherwise have charged only $200 for in your newsletter can now bring you a total of $7500.

The same holds true if you have an e-zine. An e-zine is an electronic newsletter which is sent out by e-mail. If you have 1000 subscribers and you endorse and promote a product or service which would give you a commission of $20 and you are reaching out to your subscribers and you receive a 15% response rate, that's 150 people and you were receiving a $20 commission per sale, that's $3000 in your pockets. Many e-zine owners and web site owners promote other people's e-books. The reason they do this is because an e-book is a book that is downloaded directly from the Internet into the customer's computer so that the customer can then read the book on their computer. There is no cost as far as printing or delivery, so the seller of that e-book can afford to give away a much larger percentage of the proceeds from the sale of the e-book. As a matter of fact, 100% of the proceeds from the sale of the e-book are profit because there are no printing costs and no delivery costs. So if you engage in a joint venture with the author of an e-book or the owner of a web site which sells e-books, you can right-fully ask and expect to receive a 50% commission on any sales that you make. I have seen many e-book authors and many web site owners also give to their affiliates or people who are selling their offers for them a 50% commission on what they are offering. In that situation, let's say that the person has an e-book that sells for $50 and they would be offering a 50% commission or $25 on every purchase. If you had a publication or an e-zine or a web site which receives 100 hits a day, meaning that 100 people visit your web site each day, and you had a 3% conversion ratio, which means that 3% of the people buy what you are offering, then that's three purchases a day. Now three purchases a day may not seem like a lot, but remember you're talking about a $25 commission per sale times three, that's $75 times ten is $750. Seven Hundred Fifty Dollars times three is $2250, so you're receiving $2250 just from promoting someone's e-book. There's nothing to say that you can only promote one e-book at a time. If you have a good web site, you can promote three e-books at a time. Say you promote three e-books at a time and 3% of your customers might want to purchase one e-book, 3% of your customers might want to purchase another e-book, and another 3% of your customers might want to purchase the third e-book so you're actually tripling your sales. Now you're going from receiving $2250 a month in commission from your sales to receiving $6600 worth of commissions a month. So you can see that the more products you can offer in a joint venture agreement, you're able to bring in more money. You don't have to write the e-book yourself, you don't have to publish an e-book, you don't even have to provide a service yourself, if you offer other people's products or services on a joint venture agreement, you'll be receiving a joint venture commission on their work, meaning that they are actually the ones who are going to be responsible for sale and the delivery of the book. They're the ones who are going to actually be providing the service and you'll be reaping the rewards from simply promoting their services and products.

If you know an accountant, you could offer the accountant to bring in customers for him and for every customer that you bring in to that accountant, you're allowanced fifty dollars. That's fair because an accountant charges about $150 to work with a client, so if they know that they would not otherwise have had this client, they won't mind only making $100 on the client because that's $100 more than they had before you brought in that client. If you receive $50 for every client that you provide to the accountant then you could do very well. You could set up a good web site to advertise the services of this accountant or you could take out an advertisement in a local newspaper and you are able to deliver to this accountant ten new clients a week, that's $500 a week. Remember once you deliver the client to the accountant, you don't have to do any work, you're not required to do any accounting work, you're not required to meet with the client, you're not required to do any of the paperwork, you don't have to bill the clients, you only receive a commission from providing that client to the accountant.

If you want to market the services of an attorney or a doctor, or even if you want to promote a local restaurant, you could promote a local restaurant and receive a commission every time someone goes into a restaurant and purchases a meal. There are many opportunities to conduct joint ventures. You don't even have to offer a product or service yourself to be involved in a joint venture. If you have a large database of customers, you can sell other people's products and services to your database of customers in order to make money by running a joint venture. The same is true with the reverse. If you have a good product or a good service you want to sell and you don't have a large customer base, you can contact someone who does have a large customer base and sell your products and services through that individual. Many people do this with charities. They approach charities and they tell the charity that they have a certain type of chocolate that they want to sell and if you would let me market my chocolate to all of the members who support your charity, basically every name that you have on your donor list, I'll donate 10% of the proceeds from every sale to your charity. The charity is happy to do that because now they'll be receiving 10% from every chocolate that you sell. They won't have to just depend on raising money on their own; they'll also be able to make money by having the proceeds from your sales of chocolates. You benefit because now you can reach a much larger customer base that you could not have otherwise reached. If the charity has 10,000 names on its donor list and they let all of the people on their donor list know that about your offer for chocolates and 10% of those people purchase chocolates you'll have 1000 orders being generated. If your average profit for those chocolates is $30, you'll have $30,000 coming in, you give $3000 of that revenue to the charity, and you're left with $27,000 profit. If you're just starting out in business, this is a great strategy to pursue because you're going to be able to benefit from the hard work that other people in business or in the non-profit world have done to collect a very large database of people with whom they deal. You're working on making money from the people with whom other people have already established relationships.

A benefit of doing a joint venture with a charity organization or any non-profit organization is that people might want to purchase what

you're offering simply because they want to help out the charity. Let'
say that you are selling these chocolates and you want customers to buy
chocolates. Now the customers to whom you market the chocolates
might not necessarily be so interested in the chocolates, but if they see
that a percentage of the proceeds from the chocolates is going to help
fund the charity which they support, they might purchase chocolates
just to benefit the charity. Many schools that conduct fundraisers work
on this idea. They find suppliers of merchandise such as chocolates,
cookies, candies, greeting cards, or magazines and they form a joint
venture with them. They tell the supplier that they will market their
candies or other product to all of the parents of the school. Then they
have the kids take home a flyer listing all of the products and the prices
for the products, and also let the parents know that a percentage of the
proceeds from these sales will go to the school. The candy manufacturer is happy to do this because it gives them another outlet to which
they can sell candy since they can sell candy to all the parents of the
school they would not have otherwise reached and even if they did
reach them though another form of advertising the parents would not
have responded so well in buying the candy. Now that the parents can
see that they will be helping their children's school by purchasing the
candy, the parents are likely to say that they can always use candy.
They can give the candy as a gift, they can give it to their children and
at the same time they can be helping the school that their children
attend.

You can be proactive in whatever product or service you're offering.
You could contact schools and set up joint venture fundraising opportunities with the schools. Let them know that you'll be giving them
proceeds from the sales of your products and services that they market
through the parents of the children at their school or through the
members of their congregations of their church or of their non-profit
organization or through their donor list. See there are many opportunities to enter joint ventures as long as you are creative and as long as you

realize that a joint venture really does provide a benefit to the other party. If you realize this then you should realize that they are not doing you a favor by engaging in a joint venture with you, but that they are going to be glad that you presented them with this opportunity to expand their revenue base.

Joint venture opportunities are great because most people who are in business view themselves as if they're in business by themselves and they never approach other people in business to engage in joint ventures. This means that people who are looking to do joint ventures aren't going to have that much competition. For example, if someone approaches a restaurant to engage in a joint venture, chances are that nobody else has approached that restaurant about a joint venture. So you are well off in approaching that restaurant about a joint venture because you'll benefit by being able to exchange customers with that restaurant and the restaurant will also benefit by having the business from your customers. Since no one else has contacted this restaurant, the restaurant agrees that it is an innovative idea for the restaurant you'll also be the only party with which the restaurant will do the joint venture.

Millionaire business owners are always looking for opportunities to do joint ventures because as we have mentioned in this chapter it allows them to reach out to much larger customer bases than they would have been able to reach on their own. It allows them to save money on marketing and advertising. It allows them to gain credibility by working with someone else and it allows them to gain exposure for the products and services that they are offering. If you would like to emulate these millionaire business owners, start thinking about whom the ideal joint venture candidates for your business in your marketplace whether it's a national or an international basis. You should start devising a strategy to contact those potential joint venture partners so that you can begin making money through this extremely lucrative process of joint ventures.

13

In order for any business to survive it needs to be able to weather any economic storms that take place and it also needs to be able to weather any hardships that the business incurs. One of the best ways to weather a hardship is by making sure that the business is not over-focused on any specific area. Millionaire business owners know that their business cannot focus on only one source of revenue because if that is the case if there are any challenges in that source of revenue or if that source of revenue evaporates, they'll be in a very difficult situation. Therefore, millionaire business owners know that it's very important to diversify. They spread out their revenue producing sources from more than one source into three or four different sources.

Millionaire business owners know that this diversification can help them weather any economic storms that they might face in any given area. If they have a store that sells clothing and a very large national retailer selling clothing opens up nearby, if they don't have other products which they can sell in their store they are going to be in a very difficult situation because it will take them time to replace their inventory or they could buy the wrong type of clothing and people might not like the clothing that they buy. In this case, they would have no sales. On the other hand if the store carries clothing, carries shoes, carries socks, and carries hats, then they'll have other products to sell until they're either able to replace the clothing that doesn't sell or they're able to introduce a new product to replace the clothing.

The owner of a gas station will always have a repair shop on his premises, he'll have an oil change service on his premises, and sometimes he'll also have a car wash on his premises. The reason he does that is so that if he is not able to offer the cheapest price per gallon for gasoline that he'll be able to draw upon revenue from the other services that he offers. If the owner of the gas station is not able to provide gas one week for whatever reason, he still has services that he can provide to his marketplace. Even if he is providing gas, but let's say that the gas usage goes down because another competitor opens up nearby. The owner of the gas station needs to be ready to be able to have an additional amount of revenue or be able to supplement the revenue that he or she is receiving.

The millionaire business owner will always make sure to diversify the products and services that he or she is offering. This way if there is a threat to one of sources of revenue that he or she has, there are other sources of revenue to supplement that revenue. If things go well and he doesn't have challenges with any source of revenue, he'll be making that much more money because there is a limit to how much money each source of revenue can bring in for a business. If you have different sources of revenue, you can make more money from the same customer. With the example of a gas station, there is only so much gas that a customer is going to purchase during a month. Even if someone makes all of their gas purchases at a single gas station, they are still setting a limit as to what they are spending at the gas station. If the owner of the gas station also offers a car wash on the premises people who are getting their gasoline at his gas station can get a car wash and spend an additional $10. The people who get their cars washed can also have their oil changed. The people who are having their oil changed can also have their cars checked to see that their wheels are properly aligned and can have their cars inspected at the same gas station. So you can see that the owner of the gas station is very savvy in this respect and most gas stations follow this example and provide these different services.

Let's say that even if that gas station is doing extremely well and has no competitors nearby, then that gas station will be able to make a lot of money by selling gas, offering car washes, by changing the customer's oil, by helping them maintain their cars, and by providing inspections for their automobiles. Millionaire business owners follow this strategy in any business that they own. They always make sure to offer a diverse base of products and services to their customers. Now what is important is that the products and services that are being offered to their customers should be related to each other. Otherwise the customers will get confused or they simply won't use the products and services that are being offered to them.

Let's say that you go to a gas station and in that gas station you see that there is a laundromat. You probably won't use that laundromat because you're coming to purchase gas and even if you need to do your laundry, that's probably not the environment in which you want to do your laundry. What could happen even worse is that customers could see a laundromat there, get confused and feel that perhaps the gas station is closing and that somehow the gas there is not the same as the gas at another gas station. They'll just be confused when they see two businesses that are unrelated at all functioning as one business and they might not frequent that business anymore either for its automotive-related services or its laundry services.

You need to make sure to follow what millionaire business owners do and offer different products and services that are directly connected or similar to each other. If you have a dry-cleaning store, it would be a great concept to offer machines for washing and drying laundry. You could sell soap and even actually take it a step further and have vending machines for sodas and snacks. Another step further would be to sell 99-cents items because those are items that people buy on impulse. If they walk into a laundromat and they see batteries and they know they need batteries for the walkman or they see a greeting card and they know that they want to buy a greeting card for someone's upcoming birthday, they might decide to buy it on impulse because it's available there and it's being sold at a good price. The key is that whatever it is that you offer should have a connection in the consumer's mind so that the consumer feels comfortable doing business with you and the consumer will have a reason for purchasing that other product or service that you're offering.

Millionaire business owners will take this strategy to the next level many times in their businesses. Once their initial business starts doing very well and proves to be profitable and stable, they use the resources that they now have at their disposal to open up a second business. The second business does not have to be directly related to the first business because either it will be at a different location or it will be clearly separate from the other business. You could have a pizza store next door to a laundromat and you could own both of those businesses because the customers who frequent the pizza store don't feel that they're going to eat pizza at the laundromat and people who are going to do their laundry are not going to be concerned that they're going to get their clothing dirty with the pizza that's being served at the pizza store. But if you have two different businesses then you are able to make money by appealing to different customers, by having customers who go from one business into another business, meaning someone who is waiting for their laundry to be done could go get a slice of pizza and someone who is eating pizza might decide that the next time they come there to eat pizza that they'll come and use this laundromat since they have seen how convenient it is to where they come on a regular basis to eat pizza. So millionaire business owners when they open up businesses and even if the businesses are not connected, they try to open up their businesses next to each other so that they can benefit from the customers that of each business.

Another thing that they can do is to heavily advertise one business so they won't have to advertise the other business because once they bring people into the location that's serves the pizza, they'll also have people come into their business because of the laundromat. You see if the owner heavily advertises his pizza store and the pizza store has 50-60 customers per day or 100-200 customers a day, a certain percentage of those customers will end up using the services of the laundromat because they'll now notice the services of the laundromat next door, so the laundromat does not have to be advertised. The customers who are coming to the pizza store will see the laundromat.

The same is true for a restaurant. If there's a restaurant and there's a take-out store next door to each other, that's an even better strategy because both businesses are related to each other, both businesses could be advertised under the same name, both business could be advertised to the same class of consumers, and there's no concern about confusion between both businesses. The customers who come to the restaurant and enjoy the food will be aware that they can also buy the food and take it home. They can go to the takeout store and buy the food to host a supper at home, to take the food to eat during the weekends, or they could take the food with them to have to eat during their lunch breaks from work. The owner of the pizza store, in this example, if he has a takeout, his customers will also end up taking food home. The person who comes to the takeout might decide one day instead of taking his food out that he will sit down in the restaurant and enjoy the food while sitting down in the restaurant.

So it makes sense when you have different businesses that both businesses should be either related to each other, similar in nature, or if they're clearly two separate businesses, it still makes sense for both businesses to be located next to each other because both businesses will benefit from the traffic that's created by each business' advertising and marketing or by the advertising and marketing from each respective business.

Many millionaire business owners know that it also pays to open up businesses in different areas once they have reached a certain level of success. Let's say that he has a discount store, he can apply the strategies that he has used to make his discount stores successful and open up that same type of a discount store in another neighborhood. This way if the neighborhood changes where he has his first discount store and the store doesn't do well anymore, he'll still be able to count on the profits from the second discount store. If that discount store does well, that's even the better. He'll make more money and if both discount stores don't do so well, but as long as they're still profitable, then cumulatively he'll still be making a good amount of money. Millionaire business owners will prefer to have many different locations even if each location delivers proportionately a smaller profit than having one location with a much larger profit. They know that the key is diversification because the more you distribute your eggs; the less of a chance there is for one basket to fall over and shatter all of the eggs.

Millionaire business owners are very big believers in diversification and in the benefits that diversification offers. When you diversify, you can also diversify on a small scale by carrying different products, providing different services, or by expanding into other businesses. If you're a shoe salesman, you can decide that you're also going to sell sneakers or if you're a flea market vendor and during the week you sell at a flea market, you can use the days that you're off to set up a vending route. You could spend half of the day servicing your vending route which would provide a good income and spend the other half selling at the flea market.

You can also do what I do which is to focus on the wholesale business and then look for every outlet where you can sell wholesale merchandise and diversify into different products that appeal to different types of customers. I sometimes have beauty products that are geared towards one type of store, and then I have t-shirts and clothing items that are geared towards a different type store. Even within clothing, I have different types of clothing geared towards different types of customers. Within the beauty and beauty-aid supplies there are different beauty and beauty-aid supplies that are geared towards different customers. The more I diversify, the less I have to depend on one product that I offer and the less I have to depend on one customer. There could be a point where a certain product that I offer is no longer competitive in the United States. The cost of importing the product can be much cheaper than purchasing it domestically and some of the customers that buy that product might choose to buy from importers who can give them a better price. If I depended solely on that product for my business, I'd be in a very difficult situation and soon would not have a source of revenue, but if I am diversified into other products, even if I lose that product it will not hurt my business because I have other sources of revenue from other products that I sell to make money. As long as my business is diversified to the extent so that I don't count on one single type of product and so long as I don't count on one single type of customer, I'll be able to work through hard times as well as easy times while running my business.

Millionaire business owners are very careful when they diversify because when they diversify they want to make sure that are really diversified. You don't want to sell a leather shoe and then sell a non-leather shoe because in effect, it's still a shoe and it's still geared towards the same type of customer. You don't want to be convinced of your diversification if you're selling chocolates and candies because chocolates and candies are still geared towards the same type of customer, whether it's on the wholesale or the retail level. If you're in the food business or you're in the confectionary business, you're diversified if you have very low-priced candies that are mass-produced and very high-quality exclusive candies that are not mass-produced because those are geared towards a different type of customer. You can have beverages and can have alcoholic beverages and non-alcoholic beverages that are geared towards a different type of a customer. You can have clothing and you have discount merchandise such as batteries, disposable cameras, notebooks, pens, but whatever products and services you're offering make sure that they are diversified from one another so that you can sell a different product. If one product doesn't sell well you can reach out to different types of customers so in case one segment of your customer base is unresponsive to what you are selling you can count on a different segment of your customer base.

According to the actions of millionaire business owners, diversification is the key to success. Diversification allows them to sell more and to sell more of each item that they offer to an increasing number of customers. Since there is a limit to what each customer can buy of any given item or any given service on the retail or the wholesale level, it's only logical to say that the wider variety of products and services he can offer, the more he'll be able to sell to each customer. He'll be able to increase his revenues from each customer and he'll be able to have more customers purchasing what he is selling. Instead of being able to sell only $50 worth of jewelry, $50 worth of expensive clothing, and $50 worth of expensive chocolates, as long as you have a variety of different products you'll end up selling a lot more to your customers than you would have otherwise. You see, there's always a limit to how much jewelry they'll buy, how much candy they'll buy, and how much clothing they'll buy. But if you're a source of each of those three products at an upscale level and you're catering to that upscale market, you'll be able to sell a lot more to your customers. If you wholesale to upscale stores and you only have one category of upscale products, there's always a limit to how much they can buy because they don't want too much inventory of a single product. If you have different products that are of an upscale nature, then each store will be able to order a lot more upscale products from you because they'll need to have more than one product to sell and they'll want to have more than one product to sell. So the key to your business is diversifying the products and services that you offer so you can increase the sales of each of the products and revenues that you have and cumulatively it will add up in profits. Millionaire business owners excel the growth of their business by being strong believers in the powers of diversification.

14

Millionaire business owners know that in order to succeed they do need to be able to diversify into other areas of business so they don't over-focus in an area which later proves to be unprofitable. At the same time they want make sure that they are focused in a certain area that will make them money. Since there is no concrete way of knowing which area of business will make them the most money and which area of business that will not make them money they diversify the areas with which they are familiar.

This brings us to the important topic that we are going to address in this chapter. Millionaire business owners are aware that while they do diversify into different businesses they always make sure not to diversify into areas with which they are unfamiliar. In other words, in order for millionaire business owners to be successful, they do realize the need to diversify, but what they will never do is to diversify into areas of business with which they are not familiar. We know that anytime someone goes into an area of business with which they are not familiar, they run the risk of losing money due to their inability to know how to respond to the changes of the marketplace. Since they will not know all the in's and out's of a certain area in which they are operating, it will be very hard for them not only to make money, but to prevent themselves from losing money in that area.

See millionaire business owners know that expertise will strongly influence the level of success that can be accomplished by someone. The same is true regarding the level of knowledge and education that someone has in an area. If someone expands into an area in which they are not familiar, they're going to have a very difficult time being successful in that area. Therefore, before they embark upon any business venture, they always make sure that the business venture is related to either another business venture in which they're already involved so that they can start out at an advantage because they're already familiar with the marketplace, they know the suppliers, they know the customers, and they know what responses they will be able to offer, and they also know at what price people are willing to respond to their products and their services.

The same is true when the millionaire business owner wants to start a new business or is looking into a new business opportunity. Even if that business is not related to another business in which the millionaire business owner is dealing, he will make sure that it is something with which he is intimately familiar or has access to people who are intimately familiar with that business. If a millionaire business owner has a small chain of gas stations and now he wants to open up a Chinese takeout store, he will either make sure that he has a relationship with people who are successful operators of Chinese restaurants or he'll first become familiar with that area of business. He might even spend a day or two a week working at a Chinese takeout store, not because he needs the money but because he wants to learn the in's and out's of the business.

I know of many successful business people who have spent time working at a business, whether it was retail or wholesale business, a manufacturing business, a service business, even when they didn't need the money but they did it in order to gain experience working in that business. There are many things that need to be learned and there are many things that can be learned from hands-on practice. No matter how much information you obtain from this book, you want to be able to maximize the benefits until you actually go ahead and put into practice what you are learning. But once you do put into practice what you are learning, you are going to be able to come up with ideas on your own, you are going to be able to understand what it is that you are doing and you are going to be able to become that much more proficient in your business, in starting your business, and in looking for new business opportunities.

Millionaire business owners always make sure that no matter what opportunity they are exploring or what area they are expanding that they already have a basic understanding about that with which they are going to be involved. So if a millionaire business owner wants to start a vending route and he wants to buy 20-30 vending machines to place at different non-profit organizations, retail locations, and he wants to be able to count on the steady income that those vending machines can produce, he must first learn all he can about the vending industry. Before he fully enters the business, meaning before he purchases 20-30 machines, he'll buy one or two machines and conduct a trial to see which locations are best and what actual challenges are involved when someone is running a business.

See most people don't realize the challenges of running a business until they are actually involved in running their own business. Most people don't realize that there's a very big difference between the theoretical and the practical. In theory many businesses make sense and many businesses don't make sense, but until you actually put the business into the real world by doing what you are learning to do, then you'll find new sets of challenges and opportunities to which you were not previously exposed. Millionaire business owners therefore, will want to become familiar with the business before they venture into it because no matter how good it sounds on paper, there are going to be special risks involved and there are going to be issues of which they are not aware that need to be addressed. There are going to be issues that arise which they are not going to know how to handle. This is precisely the reason that millionaire business owners conduct research and work with people who are already involved in that business so that they can see firsthand exactly what is involved in that market. And then if after doing that, there is a situation with which they need help, there is a way for them to reach out for someone with whom they can work in a certain area.

In this situation if the millionaire business owner didn't know anyone who was working in the vending industry and even if he did know someone in the vending industry and there was no role for him, in other words there was no work he could do or if the person who has the vending machines was not interested in having this millionaire business owner work with him, he could reach out to industry figures in the vending business. He could call suppliers and speak to them and see if he could spend some time working with them and ask them if they can refer him to someone with whom he can discuss the vending industry. A vending wholesaler might know someone outside of the state in which the millionaire business owner is operating so he'll be able to be exposed to the business without having the issue raised about him possibly becoming a competitor in his own area.

So what the millionaire business owner could do is to call the wholesaler and in this case he wants to vend candy, so he'll call a wholesaler who's involved in the candy business and the wholesaler could refer him to someone who does 20-30 machines in another state. For example, if the millionaire business owner is located in New Jersey, the person who he should speak with could be located in New York or Connecticut Even though those markets are different, they are still similar enough that the person who speaks with someone in the New Jersey market will have enough information that he will be able to use that information in the New York market or in the Connecticut market, or for that matter, in any market that is similar to the operating market. As long as the market has the same types of characteristics as the market in which the other individual is working, then he'll be able to give information that will benefit the person who's seeking that information.

Millionaire business owners will always seek to involve themselves with people on a continuing basis who are involved in the industry in which they are involved. The involvement doesn't stop once they start the business or once they learn the business, the involvement continues while they're actually running the business because they know that when there are issues and challenges that need to be faced and over-come in the business they might not always be able to find the correct answer. They might not always know how to handle a certain type of situation, but other successful business owners who are involved in that business might have unique ideas which they can apply to that situa-tion. The millionaire business owner might not know how to handle a certain situation in the vending industry and there might be another millionaire business owner who is also in the vending industry but he doesn't know how to handle that situation either; however, both par-ties together can enter into a discussion from which they can each con-tribute their ideas and come up with a practical solutions and ideas for that specific situation.

In order for all this to take place; the millionaire business owner knows that there are limits to the diversifications with which he can be involved. He can't diversify into a business with which he is unfamiliar. He can't diversify into a business with which he has no experience, at least not by himself. He can't diversify into a business in which he does not have access to someone who is involved in the business. He can't diversify into a business in which there is no place for him to take a role in the business before he actually starts his own business.

Now many of the things that we have discussed so far are complimen-tary to each other and sometimes when one factor is met, even if the other factors are unavailable it's still good enough for the millionaire business owner to use in order to put himself into that business. If the millionaire business owner doesn't know anyone in the business and he doesn't have access to anyone who's in the business, he could start by venturing into the business on a very small scale. By venturing into the business on a small scale, he'll learn the business as he goes, he will not be risking a large amount of money so even if the business fails he doesn't have much to risk, and at the same time since he's only starting out on a small scale, he'll have sufficient time to learn the business and examine the business as he proceeds in the business. He won't have to pay the rent with the profits from that month and he also won't have to support the business from the revenues generated by it. If the business struggles, as long as the millionaire business owner has other business ventures that are bringing in revenue then the millionaire business owner can take his time with that business and he can see how that business develops over time. He won't be under the pressure that someone else would have who was depending on that business for revenue or who was investing a lot of money into that business.

Millionaire business owners know that the best asset that they can have is information. The more information that they have regarding a business, the easier it will be for them to prosper in that business. So when millionaire business owners want to succeed, they make sure that they'll only become involved in businesses in which they can gain enough information to succeed in business and in which they will be able to have a continuing access to information within that business industry.

15

Millionaire business owners live by one saying. That saying is that in order for someone to actually become successful in business, they not only have to be familiar with this saying, but they have to actually believe in it. The extent to which they believe in this saying is the same extent to which they will be willing to work in their business and the same extent to which they will be willing to sacrifice in order to see their business succeed. Let's consider this saying.

"A person's false pride is a person's greatest downfall." By false pride we mean when a person has a very big ego and that ego impedes the person from being able to put in the amount of energy or the amount of time required to succeed in his or her business. A millionaire business owner know that in order to succeed in business, he or she will have to be involved with many tasks with which they might not enjoy and that even though those tasks might seem beneath them, if they don't involve themselves with those tasks, they will not be able to succeed in business.

A millionaire business owner who's in the retail business cannot hold himself above personally attending to the cleanliness of his establishment. If he does not actively involve himself with the cleaning of his establishment, customers will soon notice that the establishment is dirty and they'll stay away from the establishment. If the millionaire business owner waits for a cleaning crew to arrive or for his employees to clean the business, then the millionaire business owner will soon be overwhelmed by the dirt and by the grit that is in his business. Millionaire business owners know that throughout their business always must set aside their ego in order to succeed in business.

If a millionaire business owner wants to have a successful sales firm then he will himself have to spend time going on sales calls, on making cold calls, on contacting new prospects, on dealing with suppliers, on ordering paper supplies, and on negotiating prices. If an entrepreneur or a business owner feels that it is beneath him to negotiate for prices or to shop around for the best deal or to negotiate in any aspect of the business or if he feels that sales is beneath him and that's not what he's out to do, then he'll soon fail in business. Even if you have sales people working for you, even if you have other people doing the shopping for you, and you have other people doing the negotiating for you, throughout the business there will be many times when your personal involvement as far as negotiating, as far as sales, and as far as shopping will be required.

Some of those decisions will be on a small scale and some of those decisions will be on a large scale. Some of those decisions will be a matter of the millionaire business owner being out of supplies such as paper supplies and envelopes, and knowing where he can get the best deal. If he's not careful about getting the best deal, then he will soon also lose track of the larger expenses and the extra money that he's spending will soon affect his bottom line. On the other hand, if a millionaire business owner is always going to be involved with every aspect of his business, including sales, then when there's an opportunity to make money and it involves him being personally involved in the sales process, he will interject himself into the sales process in order to make money for his business. If a millionaire business owner is not actively involved in the sales process, when an opportunity arises to make money through the sales process, and even if the millionaire business owner at that point wants to help out with the sales, he has not been involved in the sales and will not have any experience and will not be able to help with that sale.

So millionaire business owners know that in order for them to succeed in business they need to be able to be involved with every aspect of their business, no matter how significant or insignificant it may seem.

A millionaire business owner involved in the construction business knows that in order to succeed, he will have to visit his construction sights on a periodic basis. He will have to wear a hard hat and actually walk through the construction site and see how the work is being done. He is going to have to keep a one-on-one relationship with all of his employees. This takes with any type of corporation, even million-dollar corporations that have thousands of employees have CEO's that will always make sure to have some type of connection to all of their employees, whether it's through an e-mail basis, through an e-mail that goes out to all of the employees, through teleconferences, through annual company gatherings, through company picnics, or through periodic visits to different branches of the company. No matter how large or how small a corporation is, the CEO knows that in order to have a company with motivated employees he will have to take an active role in meeting all of the employees. If someone felt that was beneath them because they have a high-level position within a company and that they are a big business person and should not have to deal with all of the employees on a one-to-one basis, will be violating this preset of not having false pride.

If you observe millionaire business owners very carefully, you will notice that they never feel that any role in their business is beneath them. You'll actually notice that they're excited and that they look forward to getting involved in their businesses. They love having the opportunity to be involved in any role in their business. Millionaire business owners started businesses on their own or acquired businesses with which they enjoy being involved as we mentioned at the beginning of the book. They know that since they will have to become involved personally in every role of their business at some point, they only become involved with businesses that they enjoy. The flipside is also true. They enjoy the businesses in which they're involved and never mind being involved in every aspect of their business. If a delivery needs to be made and the driver is unavailable, the millionaire business owner will get into the truck and make the delivery himself. If the millionaire business owner has a painting company and there's a house that needs to be painted and one of the employees did not show up for work and the work needs to be completed that day, the millionaire business owner will go to that house, take a paint brush, put on a uniform, and start painting. If the millionaire business owner has a restaurant one of the chefs quits and now they're short-staffed, the millionaire business owner will spend that day helping out in the kitchen until another employee can be hired.

Now this doesn't mean that millionaire business owners will involve themselves fulltime with tasks that take them away from the big picture of running their business and increasing the revenues of their business. What it does mean is that millionaire business owners are always open to solving any issues that arise, whether it requires them to be involved firsthand or secondhand. By secondhand, I mean that if the millionaire business owner feels that the best way to address an issue is by delegating the work to someone else or by hiring a temporary worker or a part-time worker or a full-time worker or an independent contractor to take care of the issue that needs to be addressed, he or she will do that. If the options are not available, the millionaire business owner will not hesitate to become involved in addressing those issues that require him getting his hands dirty and no matter to what extent he has to personally go with that involvement.

Millionaire business owners are differentiated from other business owners by their willingness to become involved in the work that needs to be done and by their willingness to sacrifice their personal image and their ego while becoming involved in the business. I've seen many successful millionaire owners who worked at the counter of their businesses because they know if they don't have someone at the counter who knows what they're doing that the business will deteriorate. The millionaire business owner will not hesitate to be involved in any part of their business because they know that in order for them to be able to reach the next level of their business they will have to be able to keep a rapport with their customers. In order to keep that rapport with their customers, they need to be able to become personally involved so that their employees know what needs to be done. They must be able to know how to encourage their employees and how to teach their employees how to relate to customers and how to work properly within the framework of the business that they are running. They know that they need to be seen actively involved in the business. The millionaire business owner will spend time working in different departments of their businesses even when they're not needed but so that they can establish a good role model for their employees. Millionaire business owners know that the more their employees see them, the more motivated their employees will be towards their jobs and also will be encouraged to refrain from being lazy and not doing their jobs. More importantly, since most employees do want to put in a full day's work and most employees are motivated, when the employees can observe the millionaire business owner being involved in his business, then the millionaire business owner knows that his employees will know exactly what is required from them and exactly what they need to do in order to succeed in the business. If the employees don't have an opportunity to personally observe their boss or the CEO of a company working in a department, they might never fully understand or realize what they need to do. Once they do observe their boss being involved in the business, they'll understand a lot of things intuitively. See, there are certain things that cannot be trained. You can't train someone to be enthusiastic or motivated. You can't train someone to have a personal connection to the business. These are things that a person to feel from within himself. Now one of the ways that a person can be helped to develop this inner feeling about a business is by seeing someone who is very motivated and very excited about the business.

Millionaire business owners become very excited and very enthusiastic in working in their business and this is because they have a personal stake in the business, meaning that this is the business that's making them money. The employees will pick up on this interest and desire on the part of the millionaire business owner. They will feel this enthusiasm because enthusiasm and positivism is contagious. The more that the employees see the owner of the business, in this case the millionaire business owner having that high level of enthusiasm, confidence, and motivation, they will also develop those feelings and the more that they develop those feelings, they will work harder, more efficiently, and produce better results while working in that business.

Therefore, to summarize what we have learned in this chapter, it's important for millionaire business owners to know that you never let pride get in the way of running your business. It's also important for anyone who's looking to start a business or who's running a business to know that if someone wants to succeed in business, the biggest threat that they will personally face to their success, is that person's own ego. Your ego can keep you from succeeding in business. If you are able to eliminate this ego and focus on what needs to be done in the business and have the full realization of how much your business will benefit from having your personal involvement with the business, then you will be able to succeed in running your business.

16

Millionaire business owners learn a lot about themselves while running their business. In the process of running their business, they face many issues and then they are able to see what their reactions are to those issues and they develop systems for dealing with issues. Sometimes part of the systems they develop to address a business issue or a personal issue is something that involves money, involves something more practical, it can involve the amount of time that you need to put into the business, or the amount of energy. It can involve the need to purchase new machinery, new equipment; to have a new computer program installed, and sometimes what needs to happen is something that the owner of the business cannot personally provide.

The millionaire business owner knows that he has certain limitations that will prevent him from dealing with certain issues. Now these limitations don't stop him from being involved in the business. These limitations don't make the millionaire business owner exit the business or look for another way to make money. On the other hand, these limitations encourage the millionaire business owner to look for other people who can help him run the business.

The entrepreneur would go ahead and look for people who have more experience than him in this specific issue and that would be able to help him succeed in this specific issue. The millionaire business owner wants to succeed and since he cannot succeed by dealing with this issue or by overwhelmingly devoting all of his time and effort into dealing with this issue, he will simply find someone else who has more experience dealing with this issue. He will find someone else who can help him with this issue. For example, if a millionaire business owner does not have good typing skills then he will hire a secretary to type for him. If a millionaire business owner doesn't have good phone skills, he'll make sure to have an employee who has better phone skills or the millionaire business owner will take a course to help him develop his phone skills, he'll hire a consultant to help him learn how to handle his calls properly and how to develop the skills that he need to use the phone successfully as a component of his business activities. In this situation, no matter which issue that needs to be addressed and no matter what needs to be accomplished, if he does not have the skills or the ability to handle this issue, instead of giving up or turning elsewhere, the important thing is to find someone who does have those skills and abilities required to address that issue.

Many times even if a millionaire business owner can succeed regarding a certain issue, he will not overwhelm himself with spending time, energy, or money in dealing with this issue, but will delegate it to someone else who can do it a fraction of the cost and do it more efficiently. You see millionaire business owners always have their eyes on the big picture. The big picture is to make money with your business and to continue growing your business. So if they lack in a certain area of skill and expertise or if they don't have a certain ability to accomplish a certain task or that trait which is not so positive for the business, they will make certain to delegate out that work to people who do possess these skills and traits. They will contract out for certain skills, traits, and services because they know that the organization or individual to whom they are contracting that work is equipped to do a much better and more efficient job for them.

Millionaire business owners always acknowledge their limitations and as they discover other limitations they look for solutions to circumvent those limitations. Those solutions could be either learning on their own how to succeed in business by dealing with those issues they will delegate the work out by hiring an employee or by hiring an independent contractor, or they will pay consultants to deal with those issues for them. Even when an individual is familiar with certain issues and knows how to deal with them, it sometimes is more cost-effective and more efficient to have someone provide that need. If a millionaire business owner is proficient at typing a letter, but he knows that it will save him time by having someone else type that letter for him, then he will have that other person type the letter. Everyone has certain skills and people also not only have certain skills, but they also enjoy what they do. If the millionaire business owner does not enjoy being an office manager, then he will hire a professional office manager who does enjoy being an office manager. This way the office manager will be a person who is devoted to the office work that needs to be done and will have the skills and expertise to solve any issues regarding that department of the business so that the millionaire business owner can be addressing the issues with which he or she enjoys being involved.

There are millionaire business owners who are involved in the administrative line of work, that are involved in providing back office support to large companies. Even those millionaire business owners once they start growing their business will not have the time to be involved in the day to day tasks of working on a customer's account, even though they themselves started out in the administrative field and they have a high level of experience in the administrative field. Since their eyes are now focused on the bigger picture, unless they are forced to be involved in the day-to-day issues that an administrative assistant or office manager needs to be involved with, they will go ahead and work on other issues regarding the business. They will hire someone to be the office manager for a certain company. They will hire their own employees to deal with certain issues that arise such as handling the back office account of a large company, but they themselves will only become involved in the issues regarding the growth of the business, such as finding new clients, making sure the clients are happy, looking for referrals from clients, developing new marketing strategies, increasing the revenues from the existing client base, and developing new products and services that they can offer to their clients.

Some ways that a millionaire business owner would be involved in a back office company is by first looking for clients and initially doing the work himself or herself. The millionaire business owner would handle the back office work for his first few clients then contract that work to other people and then as the business grows, the millionaire business owner would go out and hire other people to handle the management of the accounts and he or she would continue delegating out work to free up their time so that they could attend to other issues. In this situation, even though the millionaire business owner knows exactly what to do in this business and he or she knows how to handle the accounts, but since they want to be involved in the bigger picture of their business, they will continuously be involved in the work, other people to whom they can delegate the work, look for independent contractors, look for part-time or full-time employees, and look for interns so that they can focus on creating innovative ways to grow their business and developing lucrative products and services that they can offer to existing clients and new clients in order to make more money from their businesses. If you want to emulate millionaire business owners you would continuously look for people who can perform in certain roles of your business so that you are free to pursue the growth of your business. Remember you are the one who is ultimately responsible for the growth and direction of your business, so delegate out the work that can be done by other people and only focus on the areas in which your strict attention necessitates that you aim your focus. If you follow this type of strategy and this type of thought, you will soon see that you will be able to be productively involved in the areas required to grow your business successfully and at a much faster rate. This does not mean that you should withhold your own involvement in any area of your company, but it does mean that you must prioritize your own energies and abilities.

17

Millionaire business owners understand their true purpose in business. By the true purpose, I am not referring to their objective or their goal, but what they must accomplish in order to meet their goal. We are aware that we all have different goals and we have different reasons for wanting to be in business. Some people want to be involved in business to free up their time, some people don't want to have a boss, and some people want to become financially independent. Some people are happy with earning the same amount that they earned in their previous job or by earning the same amount of money that they would have earned from a job, as long as they don't have a boss over them. Some people want to attain millionaire status. Whatever their objective is, in for someone to truly succeed in business, that person must understand the true purpose of a business. By that I mean that they have to understand what need a business is truly serving. What does a business need to accomplish in order to become truly successful? You see 90% of people who are in business don't understand this concept and because they don't understand it and are not even really familiar with it, they continue to miss their target of what they need to do in order to be successful.

Millionaire business owners on the other hand, are familiar with this concept and they do understand aim their efforts precisely towards achieving their targeted success.

Millionaire business owners understand that the purpose of their business is to satisfy a need, not to sell a product or a service. A millionaire business owner knows that no one is interested in purchasing bikes. People are however, interested in having a bicycle which they can use to either use in their daily exercise routines, use as a means of transportation, or use just for fun, entertainment, and personal fulfillment. So there are three different needs that a bicycle can fulfill. One is the need for a person to stay healthy, one is the need for a person to get from one place to another place, and one is the innate need for pleasure. As you can see, no one really need a bicycle per se, people want the benefits that result from having a bicycle. A millionaire business owner who is in the bicycle business will understand this and will always focus on highlighting the various need-specific details and qualities of the bicycles he's selling in relation to our fulfillment requisites. A millionaire business owner will not focus on the size of the tires or on the metal from which the bike is manufactured, but the millionaire business owner will focus on the weight-loss and toning benefits or a bicycle, he is selling the benefits, not the bicycle.

Another example is someone who is selling a suit. An individual doesn't buy a suit because they need the fabric that is in the suit. The fabric or the suit is not going to a requirement of life. The reason a person buys a suit is because it provides certain benefits. Those benefits are being able to dress a certain way, but that it is not even a benefit itself. People want to be able to dress nicer for a reason, perhaps because they have to for a certain social situation in which they're involved or because they need to need to convey a certain image. If you want to succeed with selling a product or selling a service you have to understand why people would use the product or service that you are offering. When you have an accurate understanding of what people are expecting to receive from the product or service that you're offering, then you will be able to succeed.

A millionaire business owner knows that he cannot succeed in business regardless of what he is selling or what service he is providing as long as he can proportionately correspond the product or service to the need of a potential client base. People sell water in cities where water is safe and water is clean and water is healthy. The way they sell water is by stress-ing the benefits of their professed pure water in comparison with the water which the city provides. New York City's water is among the healthiest water supplies in the world, but there are many bottlers that successfully resell water in New York City because they're able to understand that people have a need to be healthy. People believe that if they drink pure and natural water that they'll enjoy better health than if they drink water from their city system which is generally just as pure or just as natural a product.

The same is true for people who are in the gourmet food business. They understand that they need is for people to not just be able to eat and to feed themselves, but the need is for people to be able to feel bet-ter about themselves and believe that they are enjoying a more promi-nent lifestyle. People want to be able to feel that they are serving their guests a more upscale cuisine and that they are more socially astute. In order to present that image, they need to be able to present the food that they serve in a certain fashion. The gourmet food business serves this need.

The same is true for people who get hair cuts. When people get hair cuts they're not getting it just to get rid of hair because there's nothing wrong with having hair on their heads. They want to appear more styl-ish, they want to look more appropriate for their jobs, they want to fit in well, they want to make a better impression upon their friends, and they want to have better relationships. There is a certain need that they're looking to fulfill. In order to become a successful millionaire business owner, you need to always be able to understand potentially the need which people are seeking to fulfill when they use your product or service.

If someone is getting a massage, they're not getting a massage because their body actually needs to have a massage. The body does not need a massage to the extent that if it never gets a massage that it will expire. No, on the contrary people get a massage to feel better, to relieve tension, and to elevate their moods. Those three items are the need that people look to have fulfilled when they get a massage. So if you were a professional masseuse and you were looking to advertise your services, you would need to advertise the benefits of the massage instead of rhetoric about exactly what you do. If you were a dentist and you were providing dental healthcare services, you would only need to list your credentials once and then instead of telling people about the cavities you fill and the teeth you clean, you should tell them about what a brilliant smile they will have from receiving your services and how attractive and appealing they will look. The same is true if you are offering nutrients and supplements that will give your patients fresher-smelling breath. You should always emphasize the benefits of having fresh-smelling breath throughout the day such as being able to attract people to them, being able to engage in close conversations, and being able to enjoy a considerably higher social advantage in their relationships with other people.

You should always ask yourself with regard to any product or service which you are considering offer how you can best advertise the benefits associated with that product or service. What specific needs will this product or service fulfill in order to be a successful business venture?

Millionaire business owners are always on the lookout for the true benefits that their products or services are providing. As a part of my business, I wholesale comic books and as part of my business, I also sell comics to the retail public. I always ask myself what benefits these comic books are providing. People are not buying the comic books for the paper because they can buy paper elsewhere and that would be silly because something which is printed or something which is prepared only to have the material benefit of having paper in their hands, so there must be another benefit and it needs to be addressed. Are they buying comic books to improve their reading skills? No, I don't think so because people who are buying comic books already know how to read and there are many other ways for people to improve their reading skills. Are they looking to it simply for its entertainment value? Well, that's partially true, but there are many other forms of entertainment, so I need to be more specific in order to fully know how to sell these comic books. Are they buying these comic books for quick entertainment, meaning it's something that they could pull out before going to sleep, read it for a few minutes, have a good feeling, feel entertained and then go to sleep? That's a possibility. Is it something that they want to have with them when they're on long car trips, sitting in an airplane for a two or three hour flight? That could also be true, or is it maybe out of nostalgia? People could be buying comic books because they want to relive their childhood. They want to think back to when they were young and these comic books bring them memories, or is it a combination of everything? Are comic books good entertainment providers because they're something with which a person doesn't have to become overly involved? It's not like having to sit for two hours watching a movie, people can just read a comic book for ten or fifteen minutes and get the same entertainment value. It gives them the feeling of nostalgia, it brings back memories of when they were younger, and it provides pure fun. It's easy entertainment, it's also a cheap form of entertainment instead of having to go to the Blockbuster and rent a video for $4-$5, or go to the movie theater and pay $10 to watch a movie, for $2-$3 or sometimes for as little as .25-.50, they can buy enough reading material to fill an hour. They can entertain themselves for that hour for a fraction of the cost of renting a movie, going to see a movie in a theater, or maybe even going to an art exhibit. The comic books are artistic, they have art, the pictures are nice, the artists who draw the comic books are professionals in their field, and the storylines are written by professional writers, so the comic books do provide a high level of entertainment value at a fraction of the cost that comic book readers would have to spend if they were looking to spend their money elsewhere. Compared to renting a movie, going to a movie theater, or purchasing a CD, which would give them the most pleasure during the first hour in which they listen to that CD could cost them $10-$11, for the same price they could buy ten or twenty comic books from me. So once I realize the true benefit of what I am providing and the true reason someone would buy comic books from me, I am able to better market the comic books that I sell both to the retail establishment, whether it's to the comic book stores, to the retail level where I sell the comic books directly to collectors, or when I sell the comic books to comic book stores who will then resell the comic books to collectors. You see even a store needs to be convinced. They need to know why they should carry a comic book. I have to explain to them why collectors will come into the store to purchase these comic books and then when they can understand why these collectors want to purchase these comic books, they can understand the value of purchasing these comic books from me to carry in their stores. So as you can see, knowing the true benefit that a product or service provides to the end user helps the person selling that product or service do a much better job selling that product or service.

The same is true with books. When an author writes a book, he can have a very high level of information in that book, but unless he knows how to truly convey the fact that he has that level of information in his book, he'll have a very hard time selling his book. Even among books that do sell, the books that have a title that convey the true benefit of the book are much better sellers than books that have ambiguous titles or titles that simply don't accurately portray and reflect the book's purpose. If I write a book on investing, I know that people are not investing just to invest. There's no satisfaction or benefit from the process of investing. The satisfaction that comes from the process of investing is produced by the results of making money through investing. When I write a book, I make sure that the title conveys the fact that this book will teach people how to invest and will help them become successful investors who can make money from their investments. The same is true with any book that I write or any book that I publish. I always want to convey the benefit of reading this book either in the title or the subtitle. When I write a book about e-bay, I want to convey the benefit of being involved with e-bay. When people understand the benefit of being involved in e-bay, then they'll want to buy a book that can help them obtain that benefit. But if the title or the subtitle of the book doesn't convey that information to the reader, the reader will not buy that book because it will appear that the book does not fulfill the need of the reader.

Millionaire business owners always look at the products and services that they have and make a list of the benefits provided by those products and services and then go on to determine who is seeking those benefits. Only after having determined these factors will they then proceed with the marketing process.

A millionaire business owner, for instance who is in the business of selling antiques will examine who are his best customers for those antiques. The way he does that is by first writing down on paper what benefits the antiques offer and what needs they fulfill. He then determines who will most likely benefit from having those needs fulfilled. If the antiques provide an investment vehicle, nostalgia, or they provide luxury to the owner of those antiques, then the millionaire business owner who is the business of selling antiques will then decide who are the best customers for those antiques based upon who needs those needs fulfilled. He will base this also upon who wants to live a fancier lifestyle, who wants to have the nostalgia that those antiques can provide, and who would want to buy antiques as an investment vehicle. When he determines those markets, then he can concentrate all of his marketing efforts in that market and he will end up selling a lot more antiques because he will know the true benefits his antiques provide, the needs his antiques fulfill, who has those needs, and who would like to profit from the benefits that those antiques provide. Once he knows exactly who is in his market, even if he doesn't do the best job when it comes to marketing, but since he is bringing water to someone who is thirsty, the person who is thirsty will want that water even if the water is not presented in the best of fashion. The reason the marketing is so very important is because there could be many sources of water for a thirsty person and you want to make sure that you are the source of water the thirsty person selects. The same is true with antiques. There are many providers of antiques and if you want to make sure that the person who is looking to buy antiques buys antiques from you, you need to make sure that you provide antiques and that you market the antiques in a fashion that the person who is in the market to purchase antiques will want to buy them from you.

So it's important to always have a clearly-defined concept of what benefits your products provide, what needs they fulfill, and how to market your products successfully so that people will know that their needs can be fulfilled by them. This is where marketing plays a very important role.

Now always understanding that you're in business to fulfill a need, you'll be able to gear yourself towards fulfilling that need. The reason you have to realize that is because people want their needs to be fulfilled and if you have that in mind, you'll always look for ways to fulfill their needs and you'll always find ways to match up the products and services that you're offering to the needs which people seek to have fulfilled. When you understand this concept, then you'll be in a situation where you'll be able to fulfill people's needs and you'll be able to provide the products and services that people need based upon their personal desires for fulfillment.

Before we end this chapter, let me give you one example with books. If there is a book that gives people a list of 100 diets, that book is obviously geared towards people who either want to stay skinny or want to lose weight. So if the book had a title such as "100 Healthy Recipes", the book would miss its point. People looking at that book wouldn't clearly see that this book has recipes that will either help them stay in shape or will help them lose weight. On the other hand, if this book is called "The Diet Recipe Book", many people might not buy that book because there are a lot of people who don't want to go on a diet, they just want to eat well so that they can stay in shape. Then the people who need to lose weight might not be convinced to buy this book just because the book is called "The Diet Recipe Book", because they have seen so many other diet books and they might have tried some of the other diet books. However, if the book was called something like "100 Recipes That Can Help You Lose 10 Lbs. In The Next Month", that's a much more appealing title. What if the book were called "Instant Weight Loss Recipes"? That would be a very catch title that would draw people's attention. Now since you want to also address the market of people who are looking to stay in shape, what if it were called "Zero-Calorie Recipes" or "Fat-Free Recipes"? "Fat-Free Recipes" would be a great title because people are looking to lose weight, it would tell people that these recipes don't contain any fat, and people know that if they reduce their fat intake they can lose weight, and for the people who want to stay in shape, it will encourage them to buy the book because when they see that there is a book that has recipes that are fat-free, they'll want to buy the book to help them stay in shape and they'll be glad to buy the book to help them trim down the amount of fat that they consume in their meals.

So millionaire business owners know that in order to succeed in business they need to have a system in place for always conveying the true benefits offered by their products and services and match those benefits to the needs of people. In other words, they're always marketing their products in a way that is aimed directly at the targeted need. They know that they first have to discover the need and then they have to clearly explain through the sales process exactly how that need will be fulfilled. They have to ignore everything else except illustrating precisely how the need will be fulfilled by the consumer's use of their product or service.

Millionaire business owners use this strategy very effectively in all types of service businesses and in all types of product businesses, in business to business, in consumer to business, or in business to consumer types of sales. Millionaire business owners know that no matter who the person is or no matter with which company they are dealing, what makes this world go 'round is the fact that people and organizations have needs and they're always on the lookout for solutions for their needs. If you can supply a solution for people's needs, then you will have people coming to you once they clearly understand how you can fulfill their needs.

18

Millionaire business owners know that in order to succeed in business, they need to be able to have a clear system which they can follow. This clear system has to work for them as an instruction manual would work for someone who is learning how to operate a vehicle or someone who is assembling a model kit. Someone who would be assembling a model kit would be very careful to follow the instructions to know how to use the glue, how much glue to apply, how to paint the model, how long to let it dry before paint is applied, and how to assemble the various components that go into the model airplane. The same applies to millionaire business owners. The millionaire business owner is careful in assembling the model and in this case the model that he is assembling is his business. A millionaire business owner will follow a clear, proven business system, whether it comes to starting a business or continuing to run the business. See millionaire business owners know that once they work very hard to develop their business system, there is no reason to move away from that business system and to try something else that might not work. On the other hand, when they have a system that does work, they are very careful to follow that same system. Even if they're involved in a different type of business, they will look at the business system that they have used before and see what they can apply, what they can't apply, and what they need to do differently this time. But by keeping a track record of how their business progressed, they'll know what mistakes to avoid and for what opportunities to look in order to make money.

Millionaire business owners use a system because a system also helps them stay more disciplined. When they have a set of parameters that they can follow, then they have rules which they know that they need to follow and whether they're in the mood to run their business one day, whether they have a new idea, or whether they're unsure of the next step, they need to examine carefully what they have done in the past and what decisions they have made. When they can look at the rules which they have set for themselves to follow in running their business, they will not have any hesitancy on their part and also even on days when they have forgotten their original plan, days when they are not sure how to progress; they'll be able to draw upon their business strategy. You see, the business strategy or the business system in this case is the set of rules and the instruction manual that millionaire business owners use in order to succeed in business. Millionaire business owners will use a definite system because by using a definite system they stay more disciplined and they're also more confident about the business that they're running.

Millionaire business owners understand that in any type of a business they will always need clear guidance; they will always need to stay focused in order to succeed. What better thing could there be than to have a system upon which to rely? When millionaire business owners are first starting out in business and they are starting a business with which they have not previously dealt, they will draw up a business plan based upon information from either experts in the field or their own research. Whatever the situation is millionaire business owners know that in order for them to succeed in business they need to be able to have a set guideline that will lead them as they are going forward in business. Many times business owners and entrepreneurs will even go as far as paying consultants to set up a business system for them so that they will know exactly what steps they need to take in order to move ahead in their business. Millionaire business owners are very careful that whoever gives them that information and whoever's system they are following has proven that system in the past and has used that system. They want to make sure that are those who have used the system and make sure that there are those that have been successful in using the system.

Millionaire business owners have a very big advantage in this respect. When they face their competitors in the marketplace and their competitors are not sure how to handle a new situation, they don't have anything to review to try to see what could be the best decision, but a millionaire business owner who does have a clear set of guidelines, even when there's a new situation that is unprecedented and the millionaire business owner is unsure about how to handle it, by looking at his business system he can receive help in making a decision. He could say "Okay, in this type of situation, this is ordinarily how I sell, in this type of a situation, I ordinarily reach a new customer, in this type of a situation, this is how I ordinarily find new suppliers." By having a business system, even if it's a new situation that will cause him to deviate from the system, he'll be able to make the correct decision in this situation by examining how he would ordinarily run his business in a similar situation. So a business system helps by allowing a millionaire business owner to make the right decision in a new situation by examining how he should run his business in a similar type situation.

Millionaire business owners use a business system in the same way that an auto mechanic would read a manual to decide how best to maintain or repair a car. Millionaire business owners use a business strategy in the same way a police officer uses a set of rules and guidelines that helps him deal with different types of situations such as investigations, riot control, apprehending a suspect, and searching for a suspect. Even when the situation that the police officer is faced with is new or unprecedented situation, he can still look at the manual that he has and see which situation in the manual is similar to this unprecedented situation. Even though unprecedented means that it's a new situation that wasn't expected or that perhaps wasn't even thought to be a plausible situation that could happen, but every situation possible has similarities to another type of situation. By comparing both situations and determining what similarities are, the millionaire business owner can decide what he should do in this new situation because he'll be able to see how he did in that situation and then he'll be able to decide what he should do in this situation.

The millionaire business owner knows that every situation with which he deals and every situation with which he's involved does have similarities to other situations that he either has been involved with in the past or situations that have taken place in business. When he can examine the correct actions and the necessary steps to take in those business situations by examining the actions and steps taken by other people in those business situations, he can determine the own correct actions and necessary steps he needs to take in his own business.

See millionaire business owners will either develop a business strategy based on their own system or will develop a strategy based on the system that other entrepreneurs and other business owners have used. In your own business, you should either set up a business system based upon your own experiences, verify that your business system does work by consulting with a professional, another business owner, someone within the industry in which you are dealing, or pay a consultant to develop a business system for you. The advantage of paying a consultant to set up a business system for you is that once you have this business system set up for you you'll know that you reliable answers and you have reliable guidance for situations that have been reviewed by a professional. In every type of situation you have the opportunity to get expert guidance by either consulting with a professional such as a business consultant or other business owners and entrepreneurs who have been involved in the business in which you want to be involved.

Regardless of the type of situation and regardless of the business in which you choose to be involved, keep in mind that other people have already been involved in that type of business and have been involved in similar types of situations that you can draw upon for their experience and apply that experience to your own personal situation. So millionaire business owners will always use a system to make sure that they are following the right system and to help them make the right decisions while they are running their business.

Millionaire business owners therefore, work hard at always developing a business system and at upgrading their business system as various situations require. As new issues arise in business and as your business changes its business environment due to government regulations, they will modify their business system in order to make sure that they make the right decisions while running their business.

Millionaire business owners also draw upon business books in order to write up their business system. They will read what other people have said about the industry in which they are operating and they will read to see what guidance they can obtain from business books, from trade journals, from newspaper articles, and incorporate the information that they read into their business system. Once they incorporate that information into their business system they have not only a clear plan of action to follow but they also have new information and new ideas which they might not have known on their own and to which they may not have been exposed. Once they do have this information, they'll be able to be more proactive in business because now they have a system based upon new ideas and new opportunities to which they were not previously exposed. So you should always be on the lookout for business books, articles, and speeches by experts in the area of business in which you will be operating and in which you are currently operating. By following the example of millionaire business owners you can develop a solid business system which can help you start your business, run your business, and expand into new opportunities to make money.

19

Millionaire business owners know that in addition to the opportunities that they have in their local market, they must always seek opportunities in other markets. The reason is because by the definition of a market, the opportunities that are in the marketplace are limited. Even if the opportunities are very large, there is a limit to those opportunities because the definition of a market is a setting or an area through which a company or an individual will be operating, or a market could be the need for a certain product or a certain service. The level of the need is the size of the market that is available. Besides the market opportunities that exist in one market, there can be other markets that the company or the organization can supply. See millionaire business owners are aware that sometimes even when there's not an opportunity available in their own market, there can be opportunities present for them in other marketplaces.

Millionaire business owners will always be looking for other marketplaces into which they can expand to make money. They know that realistically they'll only be able to capture a certain percentage of the market in which they are operating. The millionaire business owner might say to himself, "Well look, the market's extremely competitive and at best, the most I'll be able to capture of the marketplace in which I am operating is 5%." Five percent is great if you're dealing in a very large marketplace. Now let's say that you're dealing with a small marketplace and in that small marketplace 5% of that marketplace is not enough for a millionaire business owner to attain that status or to keep his status as a millionaire business owner. What you will want to do is look for other marketplaces where there are more opportunities and where 5% of the marketplace will result in your making more money in addition to just running your business.

Millionaire business owners should always be on the lookout for other marketplaces that can be served by the products or the services that he offers. They realize that as they find more markets and develop more marketplaces that they will be able to increase their revenues. So for example, the millionaire business owner who has a meat distribution company and specializes in delivering kosher meat to the marketplace. He has a very small marketplace in any city, based upon the number of people who consumer kosher meats. Now if he expands into other cities and into other states, he'll have more opportunities to increase his revenues because cumulatively he'll have his multiple revenues coming in as opposed to serving only one marketplace and only serving a very small percentage of consumers who will want kosher meats. Millionaire business owners do the same thing with a service that they offer. If an attorney is located in a very small town, he knows that there's a very small customer base for him to serve. There will only so many people who need a contract drawn, who need a will written, only a certain amount of people who will be suing someone, or who will need defense in a lawsuit. Chances are that in any small town in the United States there are good lawyers, so that lawyer will competing for a very small marketplace with other service providers. What that attorney can do is go ahead and look for other towns that are nearly for which he or she can offer their legal services.

See millionaire business owners are always looking for additional opportunities in the local, national, and international markets. They always examine how they can supply their products or services that they are supplying in their marketplace to other marketplaces. When they see an opportunity that's already related or similar to the marketplace that they are offering, they will seek ways to enter that marketplace. So for example, the millionaire business owner who sells socks and notices that there's a certain area of the country that is very cold, he'll try to sell thermal socks in that area. If the millionaire business owner realizes that there's an area in which people don't wear socks at all, then he might decide to sell shoes or sandals that people wear without socks. Millionaire business owners always use their existing business and keep their eyes open for opportunities in which they can go ahead and serve. The key in any business is to always see which additional marketplaces your product or service can serve and what opportunities arise through the normal process of running your business. Many entrepreneurs discover even more lucrative opportunities than the ones for which they are looking while they are trying to run their business.

Millionaire business owners who are in the computer business set up even more lucrative service businesses teaching people how to use their computers and helping companies set up their computer infrastructures, and setting up networks, when they realized how difficult it was for their customers to actually set up their computers. There are many companies that even charge for customer service because they realize that in addition to the basics of offering people basic knowledge of how to use their products and services that they are selling that people require a lot more help in using their products and services and want to have a higher level of sophistication and knowledge so that they can use the products and services that are obtaining in more advanced and strategic ways.

So millionaire business owners will always seek out new opportunities in their current marketplace, in their local marketplace, in their national marketplace, and in the international marketplace. If you need help expanding into other areas, you can contact the Better Business Bureau, local business groups, and Chambers of Commerce for specific information regarding certain marketplaces and what advice or assistance they can offer you in entering that marketplace.

Millionaire business owners know that networking is a key factor and when they expand internationally they make sure to contact the consuls of the country in which they are looking to do business. They also contact their own embassy as well. If you're an American, it would be the American Embassy and if you're looking to operate in another country you would contact the representative of that other country to look into the marketplace there. Millionaire business owners are always using their contacts at the city level, at the state level, at the federal level, and also their contacts in international government to help them expand their business. They realize that just as there are needs domestically for their products and services, there is also a need internationally for their products and services. So millionaire business owners will explore what marketplaces need the products or services that they're offering and they will also investigate to determine the best way to serve that marketplace so they can increase their fortunes by prospering in that marketplace.

20

In order for an individual or an organization to succeed, they need to have the trust of the public with whom they are dealing. It doesn't matter what a great product or service that someone is offering people want to trust the provider of that product or service. People need to feel very comfortable with the people with whom they are doing business before they engage in any business. It only makes sense that you would rather do business with people who you know and really trust rather than with complete strangers.

Therefore, millionaire business owners always make sure to have a good reputation. They know that if they have a good reputation that it will be easier for them to gain new prospects for their business. They know that if they have a good reputation that people will feel comfortable in referring new business to them. You see millionaire business owners believe in the strength of "word-of-mouth". They know that the better they are able to serve their audiences which are the businesses and customers with which they deal, more people they will have referred to them in business. If you're a consumer and you are very happy with the product or service that you have received from a business, you'll feel inclined to refer other people to that person who provided you with that service or product.

So millionaire business owners always want to make sure that they make a very good impression upon their customers and they always want to make sure to develop good long-term relationships with their customers so that they are able to count on not only a repeating business from that customer and they also want to be able to count on a repeating business from future customers and from future referrals that will come from that satisfied customer. In order to that, the millionaire business owner will have to ensure that they have a very good reputation. Having a good reputation is in fact, what will attract prospects or potential clients and potential customers to the business of the millionaire business owner. The millionaire business owner is in a situation where he does not always have a chance to sell his products or services. There are times when his products and services will be sold for him, meaning there will be a discussion between a prospective customer and an actual customer regarding his product or service. At that point, the customer will convey his true feelings regarding the product or service that he or she has purchased from this business to the person to whom he is speaking. Then the potential customer will decide partially based upon that conversation whether he will buy the product or service from the millionaire business owner.

One thing that is also very important for all types of businesses, especially for mail-order businesses, for Internet businesses, and for any business that uses advertising is testimonials. A testimonial is basically a reference from a customer who has used your product or service and will now be using that reference to convince other people to try the product or service. The way that you use a testimonial is by placing the testimonial on all of your literature and your advertisements. When people read those testimonials they will say to themselves that if this person was very content with the product or service that he received and if he has gone out on a limb to actually say what kind of benefits he or she has received from these products or services that the millionaire business owner has to offer, then it's safe to assume that I too will also be satisfied with the products or services that this millionaire business owner offers. So they key in business is to always make sure that your customers and even people who did not buy from you walk away with a good impression about you and a good impression regarding your business so that they will refer other people to you. In this way they will also feel inclined to give you testimonials. The best type of testimonials are the ones for which you do not ask, but are given voluntarily. Those testimonials have the most effect on potential customers. When potential customers see that you received a testimonial without having to ask for it, they will conclude that people must really be satisfied with the products or services that you are offering or otherwise that person would never have agreed to offer their opinion regarding the products or services that they have used.

So millionaire business owners will always closely guard their reputations and will always make sure to develop good, warm, long-term relationships with their customers, with their suppliers, with their vendors, and with anyone whom they deal because they want to make sure that they'll be able to continue benefiting from having these good relationships and from having a good name. I recently read in a business magazine the story of a hat retailer who sold hats exclusively from his store. At that time it was very hard for him to establish a national account with a large hat manufacturer, so he had to rely upon small distributors and wholesalers to provide him with hats. He was not able however to get certain exclusive products that he knew would sell very well in his store. What this millionaire business owner did was to continue establishing contacts in the business and ensuring that he had a good reputation until one situation arose that required him to make a very big decision that would have a tremendous and long-term impact upon his business. In this situation, he had ordered $30,000 worth of hats from a supplier. He then sold those hats to his customers, but was left short of about $20,000 to pay to his supplier. He had two choices, he could either simply not pay the supplier and find another supplier and he could declare bankruptcy, pay a small sum on the $20,000 or he could have found a way to actually go ahead and pay the money that he owed. This millionaire business owner went ahead and found a way to make the payment on his account. He set up a payment plan with his supplier and told them that no matter how long it took that he would pay every single penny that he owed. The people in the business were so impressed by the honesty and integrity of this retailer that they decided that they wanted to extend a line of credit to him because they wanted him as a customer. In turn the national hat manufacturer who previously did not want to do business with him then decided to do business with him because they realized that this individual had such a high level of integrity and was such an honest individual that they were willing to take a chance on him. You see this millionaire business owner became a millionaire business owner after being faced with this challenge or this obstacle and deciding that his reputation was very important and that he would see this challenge through to its resolution which would fully satisfy his creditor. This choice not only satisfied his creditor, but allowed him to be supplied with the best merchandise by the best manufacturer of his products. Once he had that quality merchandise, he was able to sell a lot more merchandise that was appreciated for its quality and value. This increase in sales allowed his business to grow and helped the owner to attain millionaire business owner status.

As you can see from this example and other examples with which I am sure you are familiar, having a good reputation with your customers, with your vendors, with your suppliers, and with anyone whom you deal, can only help you in your business. It will help you increase your business size by helping you take it to the next level. People who have short-term thinking sometimes look to make a quick buck at other people's expenses. The only thing that this ensures is that they stay small, that they never grow their business to the next step, and that they're never able to attain the millionaire business owner status. If you do want to become a millionaire business owner, always have your eye on the long-term and be willing to give up short-term profits and short-term situations only so that you can increase your business in the long-term.

21

Every business experiences turbulences, there are good times and there are bad times in every business. There are slumps in the economy, there are times when the economy is doing extremely well, we have recessions, and we also have economic upswings. One thing that millionaire business owners will never do is that they'll never blame any external factors for any losses that their business is experiencing. At the same time they will never actually attribute 100% of their positive results to any outside factors, even such as luck or bad luck. You see millionaire business owners learn to take full responsibility for all the results that their business has experienced. Millionaire business owners know that in order for them to succeed in business they will always need to have a clear grasp on the idea that they are the ones who are directing the future of their business.

Millionaire business owners who do not recognize that the buck stops with them will end up blaming external factors for their results in business. They will not feel like they have control of their business and when someone feels that they don't have control of their business, they will not try as hard. They don't produce the effort that they would otherwise and they slack off because they think to themselves that no matter what they do that there are external factors that will influence the success or the failure of their business.

So you see if you want to become successful, you need to follow this millionaire business owner idea and this concept of never blaming any poor results from your business on external factors and at the same time to realize from the beginning that if your business is going to make money and if your business is going to do well, besides the idea that God has control over us and that God helps us, but any other success factor that enables our business to do well is only going to take place because we ourselves put in the effort and the energy to make it happen. Even if we believe, which I do believe, that God is the one who guides us and gives us opportunities and helps us succeed with opportunities, that it is still up to us to make these opportunities take place.

No matter how many opportunities you have a no matter how many resources you have available to you, you are the one who needs to make these opportunities happen and you are the one who needs to learn how to use the resources that you have and how to use them the best way possible so that you can obtain the highest possible results from the ideas and the resources that you have at your disposal. At the same time if you learn to blame other people or to blame other external factors for the failures or the stumbling blocks of your business you'll forget that you are the one who is responsible for your business and then in turn you will not try as hard because you will be ready to blame someone else for any troubles that your business incurs.

At the same time if you always have a positive outlook about your business, you will always be motivated to find the best from every situation. Even if you're involved in a very difficult situation in your business and your business is failing, as long as you have a positive attitude you'll be more motivated, you'll be more encouraged. You will be happy and you'll be in a good mood and when a person is in a good mood and is motivated they are able to discover opportunities that they would have simply ignored if they hadn't been in a good mood or if they had not been proud of their activities.

So you see millionaire business owners always make sure to have a positive attitude towards all of their business and to always remember that they have the ability and that they have the opportunity no matter what the situation is to come out ahead. If you see millionaire business owners in action, you'll notice that even after their first business fails or their second business fails that they will always keep pushing ahead until they attain their true success. There are many situations of millionaire business owners who failed the first few times that they were involved in business, only to succeed with their tenth or their fifteenth business. We all know the story of many business stories who started from scratch, built up a large business, lost their business, only to start a second business that enabled them to reach that millionaire business owner status. So if you make sure to stay motivated you'll be able to attain the same level of success.

22

There are many ways for someone to attain millionaire business owner status. They can become a professional and develop a highly-profitable practice. They can become a very high-level executive in a corporation; they can receive stock options, year-end bonuses, and a very high salary. Someone could become a millionaire business owner by opening up a successful retail store, by starting a wholesale business, or by starting up a restaurant. Another way that millionaire business owners reach their status is by real estate.

Historically and statistically speaking, real estate has created the highest percentage of millionaire business owners as opposed to any other industry. Millionaire business owners enjoy real estate and are attracted to real estate because the effort and work that goes into one deal can result in long-term profits. By that I mean that when a millionaire business owner works on a real estate deal that for example involves an apartment building, when he puts in the work of acquiring the property, negotiating the price, of putting together the financing for that property if he has ownership of that property, the millionaire business owner can count on a steady stream of income from the rent that he'll receive from all the people who are renting apartments in the building. The same is true if the millionaire business owner buys a two-three family house. He'll receive rent from all the tenants in his property.
The same applies to commercial property. If he has a building that has three or four stores, every month he'll receive a check from the people who are renting his commercial space. The reason that real estate is so lucrative is because the owner of the real estate benefits two ways. One way that he benefits is or course by receiving the rental income. The

other way that the millionaire business owner benefits is by having the potential of profiting from the increase in the value of the property.

If the millionaire business owner purchased a two-family home worth $200,000 and every month he is receiving rent in the amount of $2000 and in addition, that same property which he purchased he was later able to sell for an additional $50,000, then he not only benefited from having the monthly rent revenues, but also from the capital gain of selling that real estate at a higher price. The millionaire business owner will invest in real estate to receive income, for money on which he or she can live, and to also be able to benefit from the potential capital gain when the value of the real estate increases in price. The same is true for all types of property.

When the millionaire business owner buys property, he can hopefully position himself to make money when the price of the property increases, or when the area in which he or she is invested experiences a stronger demand. If a different clientele starts moving into the neighborhood, then the millionaire business owner will benefit because he'll be able to receive a higher rate of rent and he'll also receive not just more rent income, but upon ever selling the property, he'll receive more money for the sale of the property.

Another great thing about investing in real estate is that you can leverage your investment. If you own a property which is worth $100,000, then you can borrow against that property to purchase another property. If you build equity in your property you can take money out of that property and borrow money against that equity to make whatever purchase you want to make next. Another example is that someone wants to buy a house and the value of the house is $300,000 and the seller of that property has agreed to lower his asking price for that house to $270,000. Now you need 10% of that amount because that's the down payment for that property and the bank will loan you the rest of the money. Let's say that the house is a three-family house and you're going to be receiving $3000 a month for rent. You buy the house for $270,000 and in addition you will still be receiving the rental income. Of course you'll have to pay the mortgage each month, so let's look at it this way. The mortgage payment is $2000 each month and the rental income you are receiving is $3000 each month, so you're making $1000 a month. You can also look at it another way and say that you're making $12,000 a year profit. Now since you've only put down $27,000 of your own money for the down payment that was required. So you have a $27,000 investment and you're receiving $12,000 a year from the rent, so on your $27,000 you're receiving $12,000 every year which means that you're making approximately 40% on your money every year. That's a great investment and where else can you make an investment and receive a 40% rate of return every year for your investment and still have the option to sell your investment at a higher price in the future?

You can also live in your property and according to the current tax law if you live in your property and then you sell your property, as long as you have lived in your property for two years, then any capital gain which results from the sale of that property is not taxable for taxation because homeowners are allowed a tax-free capital gain in the sale of their homes.

You can see why millionaire business owners are attracted to real estate and why real estate has made so many individuals and so many entrepreneurs into millionaire business owners.

23

Millionaire business owners know that diversification, as we have mentioned in the past, is essential to developing their millionaire status. Millionaire business owners like to use every approach that they can to build their fortunes. One way that they have successfully used throughout the last century, especially in this country is to build their fortune is the stock market. The reason that millionaire business owners enjoy using the stock market is because the stock market allows them to use the cash flow that they have from their existing business. It allows them to use the profits from all of their business ventures and to invest those profits while at the same time running and managing their own businesses. You see through the stock market you can take the money that you have at your disposal and can invest either actively by making your own investment decisions or by investing it passively through the use of a financial adviser or money manager. If you use a financial adviser or money manager what you are doing is taking a percentage of the money that you earning and giving it to the money manager or the financial adviser and allowing them to make the investment decisions on your behalf. Then your money can grow while at the same time you continue making money from your regular business ventures. See you're developing another source of income. You're developing basically another business venture that you can run without quitting your present business ventures, especially if you invest with a passive approach where someone else is managing your money. You will be in a situation where you are making money through your investments, or hopefully you'll be trying to make money with your investments, without having to take any time away from your current business ventures or your other pursuits.

Even if you decide to become an active investor, you can review the market after the market is closed or at the end of your regular business day or you take a break during the day and review the market and the performance of your investments. You can read articles on different companies. You can read ads as well as reports and you can make your own decisions on your investments. One of the keys to success in investing is the amount you're actually compounding.

If you're able to consistently earn a decent rate of return your money will soon double, meaning you don't have to hit home runs when it comes to investing, but as long as you have small gains on a consistent basis you'll soon find your money increasing at a substantial rate. Let's look at it this way. If you earn 5% on your money every year, while 5% seems small and in fact about fifteen years your money will have doubled. Now that's not bad, let's say your initial $5000 investment will double in fifteen years. Besides that initial investment, say every year you invest $5000, then the second $5000 which you invest in the second year, that $5000 will almost double. It will probably increase by about 95% by that fifteenth year. That $5000 you invest from your third year will increase by about 90% and every $5000 from thereon will double in fifteen years but will also increase substantially in ten years, in twelve years, in thirteen years, in six years, or in seven years. So you see as you keep increasing money in your investments and those investments keep increasing in value, things start working exponentially. Not only is the money that you're investing increasing, but also the profits that you're making on your investments, as long as you're reinvesting those profits, are also working towards increasing your overall net value.

Remember also that the best thing about investing is that it doesn't require any day-to-day selling; as a matter of fact the only selling involved is calling your broker or placing a trade online. Millionaire business owners do like to be in control, so even if they do use a financial adviser they'll keep a very close relationship with their financial adviser which involves daily communication and having discussions about the performance of their investments. It will involve weekly and monthly reviews about their investment performance. They will want to have a financial adviser to whom they can talk, share, and express their ideas. They want to feel that even though their financial adviser or the money manger is the one who is actively handling or managing their money, that they still have a role in the managing of their money.

Now remember that we have discussed compounding, and to give you an idea of the strength and power of the magic of compounding, let's look at it this way. You start out by investing $10,000 in the stock market and through being an aggressive investor, but at the same time being a conservative investor who analyzes his investments, who analyzes the stock market's performance, and overall you're able to obtain an average rate of return every year of 7%. Let's be a little more aggressive since you're experienced in investing, you have a lot of information, you network a lot, which is the same way that millionaire business owners do in business, you have a lot of contacts in the investment world, you read the Wall Street Journal, you read other leading investment publications, and you always stay on top of every lead you develop. You're able to obtain an average rate of return of 8% per year. That means that approximately every nine years your investment will double. So your $10,000 which you invest at age 25 will be $20,000 when you reach age 34. Then in another nine years which puts you at age 43, that $20,000 will now be worth $40,000. Now at age 52, that $40,000 will be worth $80,000. At age 61, that $80,000 will be worth $160,000. So even before you retire and you're at age 61, it's worth $160,000. Now let's give it another nine years when you're seventy years old, that $160,000 is now worth $320,000. All this started from a $10,000 investment which grew at a conservative rate of 8% per year. Now as we know besides that initial investment of $10,000 if you follow what most millionaire business owners do and continue to invest money and every year you manage to put away another $10,000 and that happens through investing every month about $800-$900 a month, which is a realistic amount. Remember how we said that $10,000 is going to grow at 8% rate of return, so it's growing at basically the same rate of return as your last $10,000 you invested the year before, but it's growing at a rate of one year less. Over the course of ten years, you will now have invested $10,000 because you've been a very conservative spender, you've been saving a lot of money, you've been following a good investment plan, and you've been very rigorous as far as setting money aside. Let's say that instead of $10,000 a year, you only set aside $5000 a year which will require as little as $400 a month. By the time you retire, that $5000 will be worth $160,000. If over the course of ten years if you've invested $50,000 and we'll go to age 70. Let's play it safe and say that every $5000 had the opportunity to fully grow and fully develop, so at age 79, each $5000 will now be worth $160,000. If you invested $50,000 which means you'd have ten times $160,000 which is $1.6 Million. This is not a bad amount of money, especially when the statistics in this country show that the average American retires with less than $1000 in his pocket. When you think of that, think about how much farther ahead you'll be in the game and how much better off you'll be when you can retire with $1.6 Million or you retire with $1Million or $900,000 or even $800,000. Think about how much you can do if at the age of 65 you had a net worth of $800,000 and that's only from your stock market investments. That doesn't count the value of your home, the value of your business, and it doesn't count what you receive in terms of Social Security and what you receive in terms of the earnings from your business, or from your salary. Now as you can see, millionaire business owners enjoy investing in the stock market and always have investments in the stock market because they want to take advantage of financial compounding, but at the same time we see historically that stocks out-perform any type of investment that's available on a public basis such as real estate bonds or investing your money in the bank, which means putting your money in a CD or in a savings account.

So as you can see, millionaire business owners learn how to invest in the stock market because they know that if they become an expert at discovering the best types of investments for their money, at researching companies, and at finding the best stocks in which to invest, they every year they will be able to increase their investments easily. Even if their investments do fluctuate in value and there are years that they do have losses in their portfolio, they'll have years where their portfolio does increase. They'll have a substantial amount of money in a relatively short time and if they invest over the long-term, they'll have developed a substantial amount of wealth solely through investing in the stock market.

24

While most millionaire business owners have been using old-fashioned strategies to make their money and by old-fashioned, I mean basically strategies that had been based on the strategies that were used by previous generations and by millionaire business owners who lived hundreds of years ago and even thousands of years ago. But millionaire business owners are always open to using those strategies through new and innovative ways that allow for the knowledge and development of other outlets to make money such as the Internet In this chapter we're going to discuss how millionaire business owners can use e-bay and some of them do use e-bay to increase their earnings and to mold their businesses to the next stage.

You see e-bay is an electronic marketplace that brings together millions of buyers and sellers. E-bay is basically an online auction house that consists of members who logon to the site, list their items for sale, whether they're personal items or business items, and at the same time there are many members who visit the site on an hourly basis, a daily basis, and on a monthly basis to see what items are up for auction. Because e-bay is divided among many categories and many subcategories, the members who go to e-bay looking to buy items go to specific categories, so there are markets within markets on e-bay. There are sellers who specifically sell used clothing and there are many buyers who go on e-bay to buy used clothing. They might be looking for designer labels which they can't afford when those labels are on brand new clothing so they wait and buy the clothing when it's used because they don't mind having the used clothing because they know that as long as the clothing is taken care of and that the clothing is in good condition, that they can clean it and the clothing will look pretty much like it's new.

There are e-bay sellers who sell watches and there are many e-bay buyers who go to e-bay specifically looking for watches. Now as we have said, e-bay is an auction house, so every category will have members or auctions that offer merchandise and bidders who are bidding for the right to buy that merchandise. So if you have merchandise that has a market, meaning that there are many members interested in the merchandise that you are selling, and there is not a lot of competition, meaning there are not a lot of other sellers who can offer that same type of product, and there is a strong demand for that merchandise, then you will be able to obtain a high price for the merchandise at your auction. In this type of situation, millionaire business owners will look for merchandise that other people are not selling or they will introduce merchandise that people are selling, but with slight innovations or slight improvements that will help distinguish their merchandise from the merchandise being offered by the competition. This way when they auction off their merchandise that is similar to merchandise being offered by other e-bay sellers, their merchandise will stand out and they will be able to obtain a higher price or a higher bid for their merchandise than other sellers because they're offering good merchandise in a manner that distinguishes them from other sellers.

Now because e-bay has twenty million members and some people say that e-bay might actually even have up to sixty million members, the discrepancy between the two numbers might actually be because members can different user names that use to logon to the site. Whether there are twenty million members or sixty million members, that is an extremely huge market and a huge opportunity for any person who is in business and whether you are selling a product or a service. Whether you are selling a new product or a used product, no matter in which type of market you are, there are people on e-bay who are looking for that product or service that you have to offer. Millionaire business owners look at their existing business and they ask themselves how they can use this marketplace of sixty million customers to market my products or services.

The millionaire business owner who is innovative and successful in their business fields will also look at e-bay as a new channel and a new outlet for them to increase their revenues. You should always be looking at e-bay and be analyzing e-bay to see how you sell the products and services that you have to offer on e-bay. You might discover that e-bay might soon represent 80%-90% of you revenues because e-bay represents such a tremendous market with enormous potential.

Think about a small retailer in a small town. That retailer could focus on selling expensive men's neckties, but while he is selling in a small town his market is limited to the number of people in a small town who are interested in wearing neckties and within that group the people who are interested in wearing expensive neckties. When that small retailer starts auctioning off his expensive neckties on e-bay, he now has the ability to reach hundreds of thousand of people who are interested in neckties and within that group of hundreds of thousands of people, there will be at least five-ten thousand or twenty-thirty thousand people who are interested in wearing expensive neckties. Now that's a tremendous market which can help even a small retailer located in a small, rural town in the United States reach a market of thousands and thousands of potential customers.

So as you can see, e-bay represents a vast financial opportunity for any business person regardless of how large or how small the business. As a successful entrepreneur or as a future successful entrepreneur you should always be looking at e-bay and trying to analyze what you can do to benefit from the market at e-bay developed for you.

CONCLUSION

In the course of this book you have learned many things about millionaire business owners. You have learned their strategies, you have learned their ideas, you have learned their mindset, you have seen what motivates them, you have seen their philosophies, and now you have come to the next step. In this step you need to learn how to apply all of the information that you have learned from this book to your own person situation. That might of course be very intimidating and I stress and fully recommend that you use your own financial adviser, business adviser, your accountant, or your attorney to help guide you through this process. This process is the practical application and implementation of what you have learned in this book put into action in your own life. By that I mean that you need to decide what you want to accomplish and determine the best way for you to accomplish that goal.

Now that you have been given many tools in this book, you can use these tools to help you reach your goal and help you accomplish what you seek to achieve. You see as a millionaire business owner you are always looking for new opportunities to make money and you're always looking to develop your business to the next level, but if you are using the tools and the knowledge that you developed in the beginning, you can also apply those strategies that you learned in your initial business to all future businesses.

So even if this book didn't give you a specific answer or a specific piece of advice on exactly what type of business you should start or how you should run your business, what this book has given you is the tools to be able to learn on your own and to be able to make the right decisions on your own as far as what type of business you should start and how to run your business. You see many times people learn from stages, not because that want the advice that the stages have to offer, but they want to learn what the thought process is for the stage so that they can emulate that thought process and they can also proceed and learn what they need to know in order to become successful in all of their businesses.

And now, the most exciting part is your future. Your future is where you're going to take the big step of either starting a business or even now if you're already involved in business you are going to take everything that you have learned from this book to run your business the same way that millionaire business owners have always been running their businesses and how they continue to run their businesses. You should be very excited when you realize that now you know everything that there is to know as far as running your business like a millionaire business owner. You'll know how to spot opportunities in the marketplace, you'll learn how to develop opportunities that exist in the marketplace, and best of all you will be able to make money in the marketplace as millionaire business owners do. I wish you a lot of luck and I strongly urge you to read my other book so you can draw inspiration and concrete advice on how to become a successful millionaire business owner.

If you would like to read more books, special reports, and information on this topic please visit www.DonnyLowy.com and www.closeoutexplosion.com

You can also receive personal consulting by contacting the author through the above web sites.

0-595-30723-X

www.ingramcontent.com/pod-product-compliance
Lightning Source LLC
Chambersburg PA
CBHW030918180526
45163CB00002B/375